Michał Kuchciak

German Medium Tank
Panzerkampfwagen IV
Ausf. G/H/J

KAGERO
publishing

German Medium Tank Panzerkampfwagen IV Ausf. G/H/J • Michał Kuchciak
First edition • LUBLIN 2021

Photo credits/zdjęcia: **National Digital Archives via Michał Kuchciak, via Robert Wróblewski, Kagero archive**

Cover/okładka: **Arkadiusz Wróbel**

Colour profiles/sylwetki barwne: **Arkadiusz Wróbel, Jacek Pasieczny**

Drawings sheets/plany modelarskie: **Krzysztof Mucha**

Translation/tłumaczenie: **Piotr Kolasa**

DTP: **KAGERO STUDIO**

ISBN: 978-83-66673-18-2

© All rights reserved. With the exception of quoting brief passages for the purposes of review, no part of this publication may be reproduced without prior written permission from the Publisher

Printed in Poland

KAGERO Publishing • e-mail: kagero@kagero.pl, marketing@kagero.pl
Editorial office, Marketing, Distribution: KAGERO Publishing,
Akacjowa 100, os. Borek – Turka, 20-258 Lublin 62, Poland, phone/fax +48 81 501 21 05

www.kagero.pl • shop.kagero.pl

Table of Contents
Spis Treści

BATAILLONFÜHRERWAGEN 4

VERSIONS ARMED WITH A SHORT-BARRELED 75 MM GUN 5

RE-ARMING PANZERKAMPFWAGEN IV WITH LONG BARREL GUNS 9

PZ.KPFW. IV AUSF. F2/G (SD.KFZ. 161/1) 11

TOWARDS A SIMPLIFIED DESIGN – PZ.KPFW. IV AUSF. H (SD.KFZ. 161/2) 36

FINAL VERSION – PZ.KPFW. IV AUSF. J (SD.KFZ. 161/2) 53

ORGANIZATION OF PANZER UNITS AND BRIEF COMBAT HISTORY 58

CAMOUFLAGE AND MARKINGS 70

EXPORT 71

CONCLUSION 72

SELECTED BIBLIOGRAPHY 78

ENDNOTES 78

Pz.Kpfw. IV Ausf. H from 2nd Tank Regiment, 16th PzDiv. Note an interesting camouflage method. Italy, 1943. [National Digital Archives]

BATAILLONFÜHRERWAGEN

June 28, 1919 saw the signing of the Treaty of Versailles, a peace treaty that put an end to the Great War. Germany emerged from the war defeated, stripped of swathes of territory and burdened with payment of reparations. In addition, the nation's armament programs were greatly curtailed. Germany's armored force was abolished outright, with the exception of a handful of armored vehicles for police use. All research and armored weapons development programs were also prohibited under the terms of the treaty. While initially those restrictions were generally respected, by the mid-1920s German industry began work on heavy and light combat vehicles masquerading as Großtraktor and Leichttraktor.

Germany's efforts to negate the limitations imposed by the treaty became even more evident in the early 1930s and gained a serious momentum after Hitler rose to power and became the Führer and the Chancellor of the Reich, having previously merged the offices of Chancellor and President in August 1934. By the same token he became the Commander in Chief of the Reichswehr, which in 1935 became the Wehrmacht. It was also in the early 1930s that the future German armored warfare doctrine began to emerge, championed by Col. Heinz Guderian. His concepts were an ideal match for Hitler's drive to modernize Germany's armed forces and use them as a tool of future aggression.

The future of German armament programs, including armor, was discussed at a meeting held on January 11, 1934. Interestingly, at that time two projects were already under way: a light tank designated Landwirtschaftlicher Schlepper (future Pz.Kpfw. I) and a multi-turret Neubau Fahrzeug vehicle. Following the conference, two further programs received a green light: the Z.W. (Zugführerwagen, or a "platoon's leader tank") armed with a 37 mm gun and the Begleitwagen (B.W.) escort vehicle equipped with a heavier caliber gun. Some sources refer to the latter as the Bataillonführerwagen (battalion commander's tank), since its initial application was indeed to serve in that role. The B.W. was to be employed as a support vehicle, using its superior firepower against enemy armor that couldn't be dealt with 37 mm guns carried by the Pz.Kpfw. III. It was also supposed to be used against fortified enemy positions. The B.W. was originally designed to the following specifications: top speed of up to 35 km/h, weight not exceeding 24 tons (to allow for weight limits of bridges), 75 mm main gun.

In late 1934 and early 1935 the work on the escort vehicle was carried out by Friedrich Krupp in Essen, Rheinische Metallwaren und Maschinenfabrik AG in Düsseldorf (Rheinmetall), which later merged with August Borsig GmbH to become Rheinmetall-Borsig AG, and Maschinenfabrik-Augsburg-Nürnberg AG (MAN) in Augsburg-Nuremberg. By the end of 1934 Rheinmetall-Borsig had delivered a wooden mockup of the tank, followed by the prototype, designated VK 2001(Rh), which left the factory in 1935 to begin trials at Kummersdorf proving grounds. The tank was an 18-ton vehicle with a crew of five, featuring from 16 to 20 mm of front armor and 13 mm side armor. It was powered by a 300 hp engine, which was enough to accelerate the tank to 35 km/h. The running gear – a modified version of the type used in the Neubau Fahrzeug – consisted on each side of a set of four bo-

gies with eight small road wheels, three return rollers, a drive wheel in the front and an idler wheel in the back.

Also in 1935 a Krupp-manufactured prototype was delivered under designation VK 2001(K). The vehicle was of a similar design, its suspension arrangement being the only visual difference from the Rheinmetall machine. The tank delivered by MAN (VK 2002(MAN)) was to be equipped with the running gear designed by E. Kniepkamp, featuring six large interleaved road wheels – an arrangement later used in the design of the Pz.Kpfw. V "Panther" and Pz.Kpfw. VI "Tiger". Used in the MAN prototype, the running gear was still in its proof-of-concept stage.

After a series of tests performed in 1935 and 1936, Waffen Prüfungsamt 6 Heereswaffenamt (Design Office for Armored Vehicles of the Army Ordnance Department) contracted Krupp for a full-scale production of the vehicle under initial designation 7, 5 cm Geschützpanzerwagen (Vs.Kfz. 618). Before the production could start, Krupp was required to implement some modifications to the design, which included installation of torsion bars in place of the original independent suspension. In April the following year the tank was re-named Panzerkampfwagen IV (7, 5 cm) and re-designated Vs.Kfz. 622. It was also allocated ordnance inventory number (Sonderkraftfahrzeug) 161 or Sd.Kfz. 161 for short.

VERSIONS ARMED WITH A SHORT-BARRELED 75 MM GUN

In October 1937 Krupp-Gruson plant in Magdeburg launched the production of 35 vehicles of the first series, designated Pz.Kpfw. IV (7, 5 cm)[1] Ausf. A (1 Serie/B.W.) Sd.Kfz. 161. The production run ended in March 1938 when chassis numbers 80101 to 80135 had been delivered.

The tank's running gear consisted on each side of four twin bogies with eight road wheels equipped with quarter-elliptic leaf springs. The drive wheel was in the front and idler wheel in the back. The tracks were supported by four return rollers. Both road wheels and the return rollers featured rubber bands.

The hull was manufactured from armored plates of varying thickness: front, sides and rear plates – 14.5 mm; top – 10 mm; floor – 5 mm. The turret was protected by 30 mm armor in the front, 14.5 mm on sides and in the rear and 10 mm on the roof.

Ausf. A was powered by a Maybach HL 108 TR liquid-cooled engine developing 230 hp. It was mated to a Zahnradfabrik ZF SGG 75 manual five-speec transmission. The tank had a top speed of some 30 km/h and internal fuel capacity of 453 dm^3, which allowed the vehicle to cover 140 km on roads or 90 km in off-road conditions.

Panzer IV's main armament was a Rheinmetall-Borsig 7,5 cm KwK 37 L/24 gun with a rate of fire of up to 12 rounds per minute, while additional firepower was provided by a co-axial MG 34 7.92 mm machine gun. The vehicle carried a supply of 122 main gun rounds and 3,000 rounds of machine gun ammunition.

The second version of the tank – Pz.Kpfw. IV Ausf. B (2 Serie/B.W.) Sd.Kfz. 161 – went into production in April 1938 and by September Krupp-Gruson had delivered 42 examples with chassis numbers 80201–80242.

The most visible feature of the new version was the straight front plate in front of the driver's and radio operator's stations which had replaced the step-shaped driver's compartment of the Ausf. A model. Additionally, the tank received improved 30 mm front armor, while the machine gun mounted in the superstructure of the earlier model had now been removed. Increased front armor thickness added weight to the vehicle, which now stood at 18.8 tons. The commander's cupola on the new version was also completely redesigned.

Pz.Kpfw. IV Ausf F2 with the main gun featuring a characteristic single baffle muzzle brake. Crimea, 1942. [National Digital Archives]

Pz.Kpfw. IV Ausf. H from I Platoon, 6th Company, II Battalion, 6th Tank Regiment (3. PzDiv.). Ukraine, 1944. [National Digital Archives]

Pz.Kpfw. IV Ausf. J in France, December 1944. Visible in the background is a Pz.Kpfw. V "Panther". [National Digital Archives]

A column of Pz.Kpfw. IV Ausf. Gs on the move in Rhodes. The vehicles belonged to 10th PzDiv. December 1942. [National Digital Archives]

Pz.Kpfw. IV Ausf. B (2 Serie/B.W.) Sd.Kfz. 161 was powered by a new Maybach HL 120 TR engine mated to a new Zahnradfabrik ZF SSG 76 transmission, which featured six forward gears and a reverse. Thanks to the new powerplant the tank could reach speeds of about 35 km/h. Internal ammunition supply was decreased to 80 main gun rounds and 2,700 rounds of machine gun ammo.

Pz.Kpfw. IV Ausf. C (3 Serie/B.W.) Sd.Kfz. 161 was a further development of the Ausf. B design, which was manufactured by Krupp-Gruson between September 1938 and August 1939. A total of 140 tanks were built during the production run, including 134 combat vehicles (chassis numbers 80301 – 80440).

There were only minor differences between the Ausf. B and Ausf. C versions, to the point that the two variants are rather hard to tell apart. There were only two minor details that provided visual clues as to which version of the tank one was looking at. First, the new version featured a deflector under the gun's turret, which protected the radio antenna by pushing it down when the turret was traversed. However, over time the deflector was retrofitted to earlier models as well, so perhaps the second clue will be helpful here – a cylindrical armored shield protecting the coaxial MG 34 machine gun, typical of the Ausf. C.

Hidden from view was the most important feature of the new model – a new engine mounted in chassis number 80341 onwards. The first 40 production examples of the Ausf. C were powered by the same engine used in the previous version of the tank (Maybach HL 120 TR), while later examples were equipped with Maybach HL 120 TRM motors of the same power rating as earlier models.

Pz.Kpfw. IV Ausf. C was superseded by the Pz.Kpfw. IV Ausf. D (4 Serie/B.W. and 5 Serie/B.W.) Sd.Kfz. 161, whose production was launched at Krupp-Gruson in September 1939 and continued until May 1941. Originally Krupp was contracted to deliver 200 examples of the 4 Serie/B.W., but subsequently the contract was amended to include 48 tanks of the 5 Serie/B.W. In the end 232 combat examples of the Ausf. D vehicles were manufactured, with chassis number 80501 – 807000 in the first series and 80701 – 80748 in the second series. The remaining chassis were converted into special purpose vehicles.

The design of the next version of the Panzer IV tank benefitted from lessons learned during the Polish campaign and, later, fighting in the West, the Balkans and in Africa. The main feature differentiating the tank from its earlier iterations was the return of the step-shaped driver's compartment previously used in the Ausf. A model. However, modifications introduced in the Ausf. B and C models were retained, including 30 mm front armor plate. Another "blast from the past" was a forward-mounted MG 34 machine gun. The tank's side armor thickness was increased to 20 mm, while the floor of the hull was now 10 mm thick. The hull was also widened by 10 mm.

Addition of the hull-mounted machine gun resulted in the increase of machine gun ammo to 3,150 rounds. Lessons learned in combat showed that the tank's armor was still not thick enough, which led in 1940 – 1941 to introduction of additional armor protection (Zusatzplatten) bolted to the front

Pz.Kpfw. IV Ausf. H from 4th Tank Regiment, 13th PzDiv. photographed in Debrecen, Hungary in September 1944. [National Digital Archives]

(30 mm) and sides (20 mm) of the vehicle. Addition of extra armor increased the tank's weight to 20 tons.

Late production versions of the tank featured additional vents on the engine compartment plate covers, improved cooling and ventilation systems and new air filters. Those versions were designated Ausf. D (Tp) where "Tp" stood for Trop – tropic. Other Pz.Kpfw. IV variants that saw service in Africa were also equipped with additional air filters and improved ventilation systems.

After the fall of France German plants began production of the next variant of the tank – the Pz.Kpfw. IV Ausf. E (6 Serie/B.W.) Sd.Kfz. 161. Between September 1940 and April 1941 206 examples were built at Krupp-Gruson plant (chassis numbers 80801 – 81006). Some sources maintain that a total of 223 Ausf. E vehicles were manufactured.

Following the Western campaign, new production examples of the tank received improved 50 mm front armor of the hull. Superstructure's 30 mm front armor plates were additionally protected by 20 mm Zusatzplatten, while 20 mm plates were added to the sides. Gun mantlet was protected by 35 – 37 mm armor, while floor and rear plates of the hull were 15 mm thick. Once again, additional armor resulted in increase of the vehicle's weight to 21 tons.

In addition to improved armor Ausf. E tanks received a redesigned commander's cupola, which was also relocated slightly forward to sit within the turret's outline. The turret's rear armor plate was also modified to the same effect. Prior to that it featured a cutout which was used to fit another plate forming the characteristic "bulge" under the cupola. From the Ausf. E onwards the rear wall was made of a single armor plate. The commander's cupola was protected by 50 – 59 mm of armor. Additionally, following lessons learned in Africa, the E model received a container mounted behind the turret (known as Gepäck Kasten or Rommelkiste) used for storage of spare parts.

In April 1941 the last version of the tank equipped with the 7, 5 cm KwK 37 L/24 gun went into production. Initially the order for 500 examples of the Pz.Kpfw. IV Ausf. F (7 Serie/B.W.) Sd.Kfz. 161 was awarded to Krupp, but soon Vogtländische Maschinenfabrik (Vomag) in Plauen and Nibelungwerke in St. Valentin also got onboard.

By March 1942 470 examples of the new version had been built:

- 393 tanks delivered by Krupp (chassis numbers 82001 – 82396),
- 64 examples built by Vomag (chassis numbers 82501 – 82565),
- 13 vehicles manufactured by Nibelungwerke (8201 – 82614).

Before the remaining vehicles of the series had been completed, a decision was made to re-arm the Panzer IV tanks with a long barrel main gun.

All combat vehicles of the series featured straight, single-piece front armor, but the thickness of front armor plates, as well as the turret's front armor, now approached 50 mm. Side armor plates were 30 mm thick, while the rear was protected by 20 mm plates. Rear of the turret featured 30 mm plates and the gun mantlet was protected by 50 mm of armor. The

Pz.Kpfw. IV Ausf. H and an armored personnel carrier Sd.Kfz. 251 somewhere on the Eastern Front. September 1944. [National Digital Archives]

turret was equipped with split side access hatch covers in place of a single cover used in the previous versions. The tank also received improved running gear.

RE-ARMING PANZERKAMPFWAGEN IV WITH LONG BARREL GUNS

Certain design features of the Panzerkampfwagen IV family remained unchanged throughout the tank's production, while most modifications (e.g. running gear) were largely cosmetic in nature. In general, most significant changes introduced to the design were limited to the ever growing thickness of the tank's armor, which, needless to say, was prompted by combat experience. The first six production versions of the vehicle featured the same main armament – the short barrel 7,5 cm KwK 37 L/24 gun with a rate of fire of 12 rounds per minute. The gun could be elevated from - 8° to + 20° and traversed 360°. Ammunition supply was initially 122 rounds (Ausf. A), but it later dropped to 80 – 87 rounds in follow-on versions. The following types of shells were used:

- smoke (Nebelgranate) – typically some 10 percent of ammo carried; weight – 6.21 kg, muzzle velocity – 455 m/s;
- high explosive (Sprenggranate 34 and 38) – 65 percent of ammunition supply; weight – 5.74 and 4.4 kg, muzzle velocity – 420 and 450 m/s;
- armor piercing capped (Panzergranate (KgrRotPz)) – 25 percent of ammo supply; weight – 6.8 kg, muzzle velocity – 385 m/s; armor penetration – 100 m – 41 mm, 500 m – 39 mm, 1,000 m – 35 mm, 1,500 m – 32 mm and 2,000 m – 30 mm.

As designed, the Pz.Kpfw. IV, as an escort vehicle (Begleitwagen), was supposed to provide support for Pz.Kpfw. III, whose 37 mm guns were enough to combat enemy tanks. The "IV" would be called to deal with either heavier enemy vehicles, or fortified positions, which was well within its main gun's capabilities in the early years of the war.

On September 1, 1939, the day Germany invaded Poland, the Wehrmacht fielded a total of 211 Pz.Kpfw. IV tanks, including 197 serving in frontline units. During the campaign 19 examples were lost in combat. By the time the French campaign got under way in May 1940, there were 290 vehicles of the type in Third Reich service. However, combat attrition was a lot higher that time around with Germany losing 97 vehicles. Even in those early days of the war German panzers found a worthy opponent in French Somua S-35 tanks with

Pz.Kpfw. IV Ausf. G transported on the Sd.Anh. 116 flatbed trailer towed by the Sd.Kfz. 9 tractor. The tanks had a run-in with a mine that damaged its running gear. Italy, spring 1944. [National Digital Archives]

their 40 mm armor and 47 mm gun. Equally lethal were B1 bis tanks (up to 60 mm of armor, 75 mm howitzer and a 47 mm gun) or Matilda II vehicles sporting up to 78 mm of armor and armed with a 40 mm main gun.

Panzerwaffe were in for more nasty surprises during the first months of fighting on the Eastern Front when it became clear that neither 37 and 50 mm guns carried by the "III", nor guns mounted in the turrets of the Pz.Kpfw. IV could effectively engage Soviet T-34 and KV tanks. Here is how Heinz Guderian remembered those days:

In the fight against the T-34s our armor could only succeed under extremely fortunate circumstances. Panzer IV tanks with their 75 mm short barrel guns could only hope to destroy a T-34 from behind, with a direct hit on the engine compartment protected with thin armor. To maneuver into this sort of firing position was quite a challenge, to say the least.

What proved very effective against Soviet combat vehicles was the 88 mm anti-aircraft gun. However, when the German tanks went against T-34s and KV-1 at Mtsensk on October 6, 1941, where the "88s" weren't available, they were in for a shock. When a special Armored Weapons commission arrived at in Russia to take stock of the situation, Guderian showed its members a captured T-34 tank to drive home the message that the Panzerwaffe urgently needed a new tank to maintain total superiority on the battlefield. In late November that year a requirement was officially published for a new combat vehicle featuring sloping armor, which eventually led to the emergence of the Pz.Kpfw. V "Panther".

But while the "Panther" was in the making there was an urgent need to provide the frontline troops with a weapon that could level the field on the Eastern Front. To that end in early 1942 German tank crews began to receive HEAT rounds. This type of ammunition didn't require high initial muzzle velocities and was equally effective at 100, 500, 1,000 or 1,500 m. 75 mm guns mounted in the turrets of Panzer IVs could fire the following types of HEAT rounds:

- Gr38Hl (Granate 1938 mit Hohlladung): weight – 4.5 kg, muzzle velocity – 452 m/s, armor penetration – 45 mm;

- Gr38Hl/A: weight – 4.4 kg, muzzle velocity – 450 m/s, armor penetration – 75 mm;

- Gr38Hl/B: weight – 4.57 kg, muzzle velocity – 450 m/s, armor penetration – 75 mm;

- Gr38Hl/C: weight – 4.8 kg, muzzle velocity – 450 m/s, armor penetration – 100 mm.

This PzKpfw IV resting in the rubble was destroyed by Polish 4th Tank Regiment "Skorpion". [National Digital Archives]

In addition, in early 1941 work began on comprehensive re-arming of the tanks in frontline service. The approach to that task was two-pronged: first, a single Pz.Kpfw. IV Ausf. D was fitted with a 5 cm KwK 39 L/60 gun. Following Hitler's approval of the project, Krupp received a preliminary contract to build 80 vehicles armed with the new gun.

Then, on November 18, 1941 Heereswaffenamt contracted Krupp and Rheinmetall-Borsig to design a 75 mm tank gun with a long barrel, i.e. producing higher muzzle velocities. The new design, designated 7,5 cm KwK 40 L/43, was to be based on the 7,5 cm Pak 40 L/46 towed anti-tank weapon. The gun featured a characteristic single-chamber muzzle brake. Full-scale production of the weapon was launched in March 1942. As soon as the guns became available they were mounted in Pz.Kpfw. Ausf. F rolling off the production lines. Re-armed tanks received a new designation - Pz.Kpfw. IV Ausf. F2 (7b Serie/B.W.). In early 1943 25 examples of Pz.Kpfw. IV Ausf. F (F1) also received the new gun. In the end, the initial idea of arming the "IV" with a 50 mm KwK 39 L/60 gun was abandoned in favor of the 75 mm weapon. The former was eventually used to re-arm Pz.Kpfw. IIIs.

Table 1. Comparison of guns used in Pz.Kpfw. IV tanks			
	7,5 cm KwK 37 L/24	7,5 cm KwK 40 L/43	7,5 cm KwK 40 L/48
Caliber	75 mm	75 mm	75 mm
Barrel length	1,766 mm	3,218 mm	3,615 mm
Rate of fire	up to 12 rpm	10-15 rpm	10-15 rpm
Elevation	- 8° to + 20°	- 8° to + 20°	- 8° to + 20°
Azimuth	360° (turret traverse)	360° (turret traverse)	360° (turret traverse)
Ammunition supply	64 rounds	87 rounds	87 rounds

PZ.KPFW. IV AUSF. F2/G (SD.KFZ. 161/1)

For a number of years sources dealing with the subject of German armored vehicles have been circulating information (often contradictory, especially when it comes to factory serials) that the re-armed version of the Pz.Kpfw. IV Ausf. F was designated Ausf. F2 and that 175 examples of the vehicle were built in three different plants:

- Krupp-Gruson in Magdeburg delivered 54 tanks (chassis numbers 82396 – 82500);
- Vogtländische Maschinenfabrik (Vomag) in Plauen built 110 tanks (82566 – 82675);
- Nibelungwerke in St. Valentin manufactured 11 examples (82615 – 82625).

www.kagero.eu

The next version of the "IV" – Ausf. G was manufactured between May 1942 and June 1943. A total of 1,750 examples of the tank were originally ordered, but only 1,687 were built (chassis numbers 82651 – 84400). Some sources maintain that the chassis numbers were in fact 82701 – 84400. The tanks were built in the following locations:
- Krupp-Gruson – 600 vehicles;
- Nibelungwerke – 350 examples;
- Vomag – 300 tanks.

The remaining chassis were used to build a range of derivative vehicles.

However, new research seems to suggest a different version. It is true that the Pz.Kpfw. IV Ausf. F armed with the KwK 40 gun went into production in March 1942 and initially received the Pz.Kpfw. IV Ausf. F-Umbau designation (umbau – rebuilt), which was later changed to Pz.Kpfw. IV Ausf. F2 Sd.Kfz. 161/1. When the Ausf. F2 version went into production, the previous variant, armed with the KwK 37 gun, was renamed Pz.Kpfw. IV Ausf. F1. As future would show, the re-armed Pz.Kpfw. IV was transformed from a support vehicle into the mainstay of German armored forces.

As mentioned earlier, a total of 175 examples of the Pz.Kpfw. IV Ausf. F2 went into service with the Panzerwaffe. In addition, 25 Ausf. F1 tanks were also re-armed with long barrel guns in early 1943. The new machines were manufactured by Krupp-Gruson, Vomag and Nibelungwerke.

The new version, similarly to the Ausf. F1 machines, featured improved 50 mm front armor. Armor protection of the vehicles was as follows:
- front superstructure – 50 mm plate, sloped at 8° in relation to horizontal plane;
- front sloped armored hull plate – 20 mm, sloped at 72°;
- front middle hull plate – 50 mm, sloped at 14°;
- front lower hull plate – 30 mm, sloped at 61°;
- side plates – 30 mm (0°) and 20 mm (rear section, sloped at 10°);
- upper rear hull plate – 20 mm, sloped at 10°;
- middle rear hull plate – 20 mm, sloped at 10°;
- lower rear hull plate – 14.5 mm, sloped at 74°;

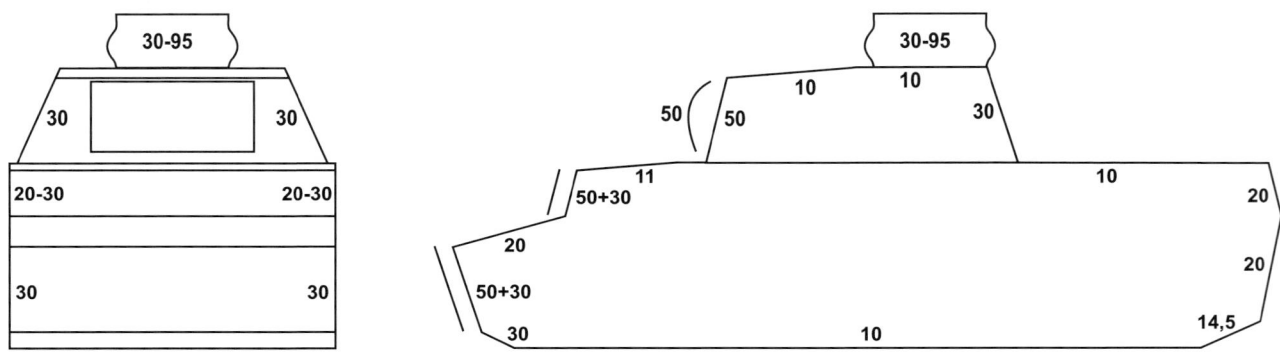

Armor protection arrangement of the Pz.Kpfw. IV Ausf. G. [Drawing by M. Kuchciak]

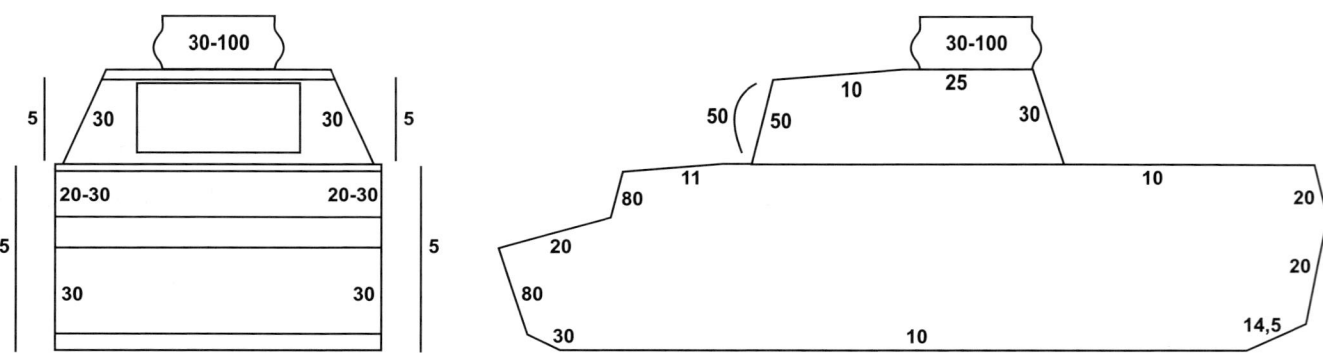

Armor protection arrangement of the Pz.Kpfw. IV Ausf. H (including Schürzen). [Drawing by M. Kuchciak]

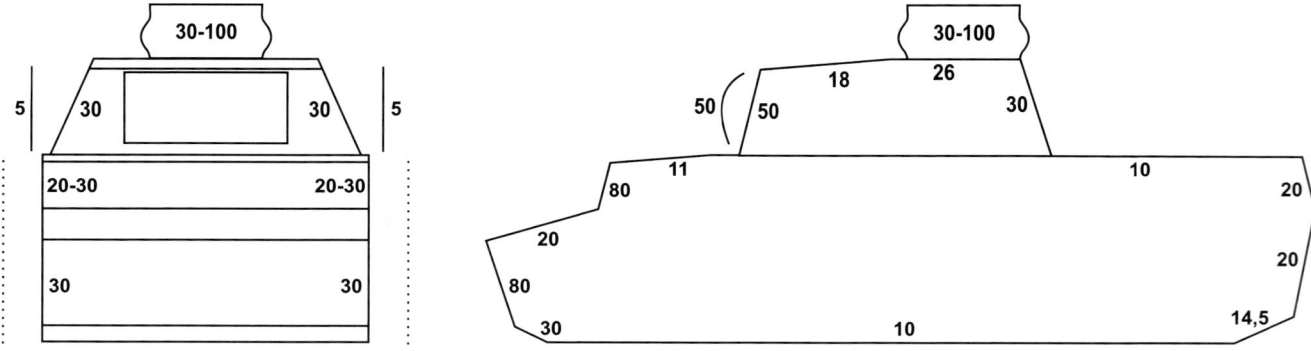

Armor protection arrangement of the Pz.Kpfw. IV Ausf. J (including Schürzen). [Drawing by M. Kuchciak]

Knocked out Pz.Kpfw. IV Ausf. H or J from an unknown unit. Notice Zimmerit coating and spare track links on the glacis. [Kagero archives]

A commemorative photo in front of a knocked out Pz.Kpfw. IV Ausf. G. [Kagero archives]

- roof – 10 – 11 mm, 85 - 90°
- floor – 10 mm, 90°.

The tank's hull housed a driving compartment in the front, fighting compartment just behind it and the engine compartment in the back. The driver sat on the left side of the driving compartment with radio operator's station to his right. Planetary Zahnradfabrik Friedrichshafen SSG (Synchronisiert Sechs-Gang) 76 transmission sat between those two crew stations. The transmission featured six forward gears and a single reverse gear. Depending on the gear selected, the tank could reach the following speeds:

- 1 – 4.7 km/h,
- 2 – 9.9 km/h,
- 3 – 15.2 km/h,

This "IV" was lost somewhere on the Western Front. [Kagero archives]

This destroyed Panzer IV was equipped with turret spaced armor, but side skirts were most likely never installed. [Kagero archives]

The same tank, this time being inspected by U.S. troops. Notice a Jeep parked in the background. [Kagero archives]

This Pz.Kpfw. IV Ausf. H or J from an unknown unit was abandoned in this burnt-out town. [Kagero archives]

An American GI taking a closer look at a Panzer IV abandoned somewhere in the West. The tank didn't have the side spaced armor plates. [Kagero archives]

Two U.S. soldiers pose on the turret of a Pz.Kpfw. IV Ausf. H or J. The tank features all-steel return rollers. [Kagero archives]

Another photo op with a Pz.Kpfw. IV Ausf. J from an unknown unit. Shown to good advantage are vertical exhaust stacks and wire mesh screens protecting the vehicle's sides, also known as Thoma Schürzen. [Kagero archives]

- 4 – 23.0 km/h,
- 5 – 32.6 km/h,
- 6 – 42.0 km/h,
- reverse – 5.8 km/h.

Mounted in the front armor plate in front of the driver was the Fahrersehklappe 50 vision port, where the numeral corresponded to the thickness of the plate for which the port was designed. Under combat conditions the driver could use twin-lens Fahreroptik KFF 2 periscope providing a 65° field of vision. The periscope was mounted in the hatch cover above the driver's seat.

The radio operator manned the Funkgerät (FuG) 5 radio mounted on the transmission housing. The radio consisted of a 10W 10 W.S.c transmitter and a Ukw.E.e receiver. The radio's effective range when the vehicle was stationary was 6.4 km (voice) or 9.4 km (Morse). Operating frequency range was 27.2 – 33.3 MHz. A two-meter rod antenna was attached to the right side of the hull. When not in use, the antenna could be stowed in a wooden box mounted on the same side of the tank. A 12 V electrical system drew power from two 600W Bosch GTLN 600/12-150 generators or from a bank of four 12V Bosch 12B 105 batteries with the capacity of 105 Amp hours. Electrical power was supplied to the radio, driver dashboard instruments, horn, ventilator, two mud guard-mounted lights and firing mechanisms for the main gun and machine guns.

The radio operator was also in charge of the forward-mounted 7.92 mm MG 34 machine gun. The gun, mounted in the Kugellblende 50 designed for a 50 mm armor plate, had a rate of fire of 900 rpm and muzzle velocity of 755 m/s. It could be trained left and right up to 15°, 15° up and up to 10° down. The gun was equipped with Kugelzielfernrohr (KgZF) 2 gun sight manufactured by Carl Zeiss, which provided 1.8 magnification and 18° field of view.

Both crew members sitting in the front were provided with single-cover hatches above their seats and Sehklappe 30 vision ports on the side walls. A 440 mm emergency escape hatch was located in the tank's floor behind the radio operator's station. The section of the front armor plate covering final drive components was equipped with two hinged inspection hatches with ventilation slits. There was also a square opening covered with a bolted on cover. The front plate of the armored hull featured two towing C-hooks, while the rear plate had a towing mount with the exhaust muffler just above it. Spare track links carried on the front of the hull provided additional protection. Stowed on the mud guards were tool kits and digging

Pz.Kpfw. IV Ausf. H/J from III Platoon, 6th Company of an unidentified unit. The vehicle is equipped with full spaced armor. [Kagero archives]

Pz.Kpfw. IV Ausf. H/J from I Platoon 2nd Company of an unidentified unit. Notice track links mounted by the crew not only on the glacis, but also on the front superstructure plate and on the front of the turret. [Kagero archives]

Knocked out Pz.Kpfw. IV Ausf. H/J from an unidentified unit. The vehicle is covered with Zimmerit compound and features all-steel return rollers. [Kagero archives]

Pz.Kpfw. IV Ausf. J from an unidentified unit, abandoned somewhere on the Western Front. Steel wire mesh screens protecting the vehicle's sides can be clearly seen. [Kagero archives]

Another commemorative photo in front of a knocked out Panzer IV. Notice the additional armor plate attached to the superstructure's front armor. [Kagero archives]

tools. In a separate stowage box on the left mud guard one could find spare parts and a hand-operated fuel pump. A jack was stowed in a box carried on the right mud guard. Collapsible cleaning rod for the main gun was stowed above the left engine air intake.

The tank's hexagonal turret sat on top of the fighting compartment in a turret ring measuring 1,680 mm in diameter. Due to the arrangement of traversing mechanism in the superstructure, the turret was offset by 51.7 mm to the left from the vehicle's centerline. The turret could be electrically traversed at 14° per second (a full rotation in 26 seconds) or at 1.9° - 2.6° if operated manually using gunner's or loader's hand cranks. The turret was constructed of armor plates welded to the steel frame:

This Pz.Kpfw. IV Ausf. H or J "524" used to belong to II Platoon, 5th Company of unknown unit. Shown to a good advantage is the Zimmerit-covered rear hull. [Kagero archives]

The same tank being inspected by U.S. troops. Western Front. [Kagero archives]

- front plate – 50 mm, sloped at 10° in relation to the vertical plane;
- gun mantlet – 50 mm;
- side plates – 35 mm, 25°;
- curved rear plate – 30 mm, 14° - 26°;
- roof – 10 mm, 90° and 84°.

Each of the turret's forward side walls was equipped with a vision port. Behind them there were crew access hatches with split covers. In the forward part of each access hatch cover there was a slit observation port protected by armored glass, while the aft portion of the cover had a gun port covered with a metal flap. Above the access hatch was a rain gutter, while handholds facilitating entry into the vehicle were welded to the turret's roof.

The turret housed three crew stations: the loader was sitting on the right side of the turret, gunner was to his left,

Crew members take a break on top of their Pz.Kpfw. IV Ausf. H featuring all-steel return rollers. Eastern Front, September 1944. [National Digital Archives]

Pz.Kpfw. IV Ausf. G with the running gear damaged by a mine being transported on a Sd.Anh. 116 flatbed trailer towed by a Sd.Kfz. 9 tractor. Italy, spring 1944. [National Digital Archives]

Abandoned Pz.Kpfw. IV Ausf. H being inspected by U.S. troops. Note a Sherman parked in the background on the left hand side. [Kagero archives]

This is most likely the same tank before it was pulled out of the mud pit where it got stuck. [Kagero archives]

while the tank's commander sat behind him. At the commander's disposal was the cupola with five observation ports covered with a spilt hatch. The cupola was protected by 95 mm of armor.

The turret's front plate also featured two observation ports covered with metal flaps. Additionally, a pair of gun ports was provided in the rear wall of the turret. A ventilator was installed in the roof of the turret, while hoisting hooks were welded to the turret's sides. Behind the turret was a stowage container for spare parts (Gepäck Kasten or Rommelkiste), which was introduced following combat lessons learned in North Africa.

The tank's main armament was the 7,5 cm KwK 40 L/43 gun with a 43 caliber barrel (around 3,218 mm), which featured a characteristic ball-shaped single-chamber muzzle brake. Since the muzzle brake caused some issues with the proper balancing of the barrel, the gun's hydraulic recoil mechanism was placed on the right side of the turret. Most tanks also featured a metal deflector under the barrel to protect the antenna while the turret was traversing. This addition was often removed in the field by tank crews. The gun had a rate of fire 10 – 15 rounds per minute and a range of 7,700 m. The barrel could be elevated from -8° to +20° and traversed the full 360°. The gunner was provided with a Turmzielfernrohr TzF 5f or 5f/1 telescopic gun sight offering x2.5 magnification and a 24° field of vision. The sight was zeroed at 1,500 m for PzGr. 40, 2,500 m for PzGr. 39 and 3,000 for HE rounds.

The tank carried a supply of 87 rounds for the main gun: 55 stowed in the fighting compartment and 32 in the turret. The gun could fire the following types of ammunition:

- HE rounds (Sprenggranate 34): weight – 5.74 kg, muzzle velocity 500 m/s;
- armor piercing rounds (Panzergranate 39): weight – 6.8 kg, muzzle velocity 750 m/s; at 100 m the round could penetrate 99 mm of armor, 91 mm at 1,000 m or 63 mm at 2,000 m;

Pz.Kpfw. IV Ausf. G from an unknown unit. Notice jerry cans on the turret. [Kagero archives]

A keepsake photo in front of a knocked out Pz.Kpfw. IV Ausf. J. [Kagero archives]

A U.S. soldier posing in the commander's cupola of a Pz.Kpfw. IV Ausf. H "613". The vehicle is covered with Zimmerit compound. [Kagero archives]

- APCR rounds (Panzergranate 40) - projectile with a sub-caliber tungsten core: weight – 4.1 kg, muzzle velocity – 930 m/s, armor penetration: 108 mm at 500 m, 85 mm at 1,000 m, 52 mm at 2,000 m;
- HEAT rounds - Gr38Hl/A (Granate 1938 mit Hohlladung Ausf. A), Gr38Hl/B and Gr38Hl/C: muzzle velocity: 450 m/s, weight: 4.4 kg, 4.57 kg and 4.8 kg, armor penetration: 70, 75 and 100 mm;
- smoke shells (Nebelgranate) – muzzle velocity: 540 m/s.

The tank was also armed with a coaxial MG 34 machine gun, as well as the forward-mounted MG 34. The supply of ammunition for both machine guns was 3,150 rounds stowed

Burning Pz.Kpfw. IV Ausf. H or J "211" from an Unknown unit. [Kagero archives]

Destroyed Pz.Kpfw. IV Ausf. H or J. The tank was equipped with a set of side skirts and turret Schürzen. [Kagero archives]

Destroyed Pz.Kpfw. IV Ausf. H or J from an unknown unit. The tank was equipped with a set of side skirts and turret Schürzen. [Kagero archives]

Pz.Kpfw. IV Ausf. H from 12th SS Tank Regiment (12th PzDiv. SS „Hitlerjugend") during fighting at Rouen, June 21, 1944. This is an early production model featuring rubber-rimmed return rollers, additional armor (Zusatzpanzerung) on the hull's front and Zimmerit coating. Notice the hull-mounted MG 34 machine gun is missing. [Bundesarchiv]

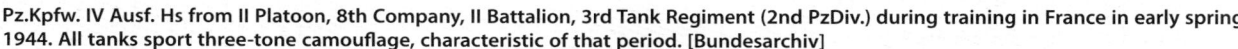

The crew of this Pz.Kpfw. IV Ausf. H from 2nd Company, I Battalion, 8th Tank Regiment (15th PzDiv.) are repairing the tank's track under fire. Monte Cassino area, early spring 1944. In January of 1944 the unit had 22 vehicles of that type. [Bundesarchiv]

Pz.Kpfw. IV Ausf. Hs from II Platoon, 8th Company, II Battalion, 3rd Tank Regiment (2nd PzDiv.) during training in France in early spring 1944. All tanks sport three-tone camouflage, characteristic of that period. [Bundesarchiv]

This early production example of the Pz.Kpfw. IV Ausf. H features rubber-rimmed return rollers and Zusatzpanzerung. Side Schürzen and their supports were probably removed in the field. Italian campaign, early 1944. [Bundesarchiv]

in 21 magazines, 150 rounds per magazine. The crew also carried 9 mm pistols, as well as an MP-38 or MP-40 submachine guns with a supply of 198 rounds of ammunition. With a new gun and increased supply of ammunition the tank's combat weight went up to 23.6 tons.

The tank was powered by Maybach 120 TRM – a four-stroke, carbureted, liquid-cooled, twelve-cylinder OHV engine. It was installed in the engine compartment separated from the fighting compartment by a firewall, which featured two ports allowing access to the engine and its ancillaries. The engine produced 265 hp at 2,600 rpm. It had a compression ratio of 6.5:1 and a cylinder bore of 105 mm. The piston stroke was 115 mm and engine capacity 11,867 cm³. The engine used 74 octane gasoline which was carried in three fuel tanks mounted in the fighting compartment: 140 l, 110 l and 220 l, for a total of 470 l. Onboard fuel allowed the vehicle to travel 200 km on road surfaces or 130 km in off-road conditions.

The tank's fuel system consisted of two engine-driven Solex fuel pumps and an emergency hand pump. A pair of 24 V, 4 hp Bosch BNG 4/24 CRS 178 starter motors were used for normal engine start, but an emergency Bosch AL/ZM 1 inertial starter was also available. The engine good also be crank-started using a crank placed in a socket in the rear armor plate. The tanks operating in harsh winter conditions of the Eastern Front used an ingenious system called Kühl-wasserübertragung. The idea behind it was pumping engine coolant from a running engine of one tank into the engine of another tank that needed to be cranked up.

The cooling system of Panzer IV vehicles consisted of a pair of radiators placed on each side of the engine compartment, behind the engine. Two large fans placed above the Maybach on the right hand side provided air circulation throughout the engine compartment. Air intake and exhaust were placed on the sides of the rear part of the hull. The armored engine cover featured inspection ports allowing access to the engine. As has been mentioned earlier, all Pz.Kpfw. IVs deployed to North Africa were equipped with tropical air filters and improved cooling systems.

Increased weight of the vehicle required the use of new, wider tracks of single-link and single-pin design, which were supposed to better distribute the tank's weight. Those magnesium steel units, designated Kgs. 61/400/120, were 400 mm wide, had a resistance length of 3,720 mm, consisted of 99 links and had a track base of 2,450 mm. The tank's running gear consisted of eight road wheels on each side (470x75-660) arranged in four

Pz.Kpfw. IV Ausf. H from III Platoon, 6th Company, II Battalion, 12th SS Tank Regiment (12. PzDiv. SS "Hitlerjugend") during training in Belgium. Zimmerit had been applied to the front hull plates, front turret armor, upper armor skirts and mud guards. Spare track links served as additional protection of the tank's front section. November/December 1943. [Bundesarchiv]

Pz.Kpfw. IV Ausf. H from II Platoon, 6th Company, II Battalion 12th SS Tank Regiment (12th PzDiv. SS "Hitlerjugend"). Beverloo area, early 1944. [Bundesarchiv]

Pz.Kpfw. IV Ausf. H from I Platoon, 6th Company, II Battalion, 12th SS Tank Regiment (12th PzDiv. SS "Hitlerjugend"). Beverloo area, early 1944. [Bundesarchiv]

Early production example of the Pz.Kpfw. IV Ausf. H from I Battalion, 35th Tank Regiment, 4th PzDiv. Most likely Dmitrovsk area, September 1943. [Bundesarchiv]

Pz.Kpfw. IV Ausf. H from III Platoon, 1st Company, I Battalion, 35th Tank Regiment (4th PzDiv.). The vehicle had been whitewashed using removable white paint. Bobruisk area, early 1944. [Bundesarchiv]

This brand-new, early production Pz.Kpfw. IV Ausf. H was photographed shortly after it had been delivered to the front. The vehicle features standard factory-applied paint scheme and no tactical markings, which would be later applied in the field. Eastern Front, July or August 1943. [Bundesarchiv]

twin bogies with quarter-elliptic leaf springs. Drive wheels were located in the front, while welded idler wheels were installed in the back. Four return rollers measured 250x65-135. Both return rollers and road wheels were rubber-rimmed. Mechanical Krupp brakes were attached to the tank's drive wheels.

The vehicle was manufactured under the Pz.Kpfw. IV Ausf. F2 designation for three months. In June 1942 the designation was changed to Pz.Kpfw. IV Ausf. G (8 Serie/B.W.) Sd.Kfz. 161/1. In total 1,930 examples of the Pz.Kpfw. IV Ausf F2/G were built between March 1942 and June 1943 (includ-

Pz.Kpfw. IV Ausf. H or Ausf. J from 6th Company of an unidentified Panzerwaffe unit fighting in Poland in August 1944. Note additional makeshift armor consisting of Soviet T-34 track links. [Bundesarchiv]

This damaged Pz.Kpfw. IV Ausf. H from 8th Company, II Battalion, 29th Tank Regiment (12th PzDiv.) is being prepared for evacuation. In front of the tank is a Zugkraftwagen 18t Sd.Kfz. 9 heavy half-track tractor. The photo was taken on July 19, 1944 in Bialystok, Poland. [Bundesarchiv]

Pz.Kpfw. IV Ausf. H fighting on the Eastern Front in early 1944. [Bundesarchiv]

A series of photographs showing a platoon of Pz.Kpfw. IV Ausf. H tanks from an unknown Wehrmacht unit fighting on the Eastern Front in January/February 1944. All vehicles carry spare track links on the glacis. [Bundesarchiv]

A series of photographs showing a platoon of Pz.Kpfw. IV Ausf. H tanks from an unknown Wehrmacht unit fighting on the Eastern Front in January/February 1944. All vehicles carry spare track links on the glacis. [Bundesarchiv]

ing 175+25 examples with the interim designation Ausf. F2) with chassis numbers 82394 – 84400. Production was split between the following locations:
- Krupp-Gruson – 907 vehicles;
- Nibelungwerke – 587 machines;
- Vomag – 346 tanks.

The remaining chassis were used for a number of derivative vehicles.

As the production went on, numerous modifications were introduced into the tank's design. One of them was a new gun – the 7,5 cm KwK 40 L/48 – which began to arrive at assembly lines in April 1943. Also, the "IVs" undergoing factory overhauls between 1942 and 1943 (mainly Ausf. D and E models) were routinely retrofitted with Ausf. G turrets with long barrel guns. Another modification, introduced a bit earlier – in February 1943 – was the increase of the armor protection of the commander's cupola to 100 mm. At around the same time the split hatch covers were replaced with single-piece units. Another addition was a pair of triple smoke grenade launchers mounted on either side of the turret. Starting in July 1942 the tanks received additional 30 mm armor (Zusatzplatten), which were either bolted or welded to the front of the hull.

Other changes included the disappearance of the observation ports on the tank's turret sidewalls (beginning with Ausf.

Pz.Kpfw. IV Ausf. H vehicles from an unidentified unit during fighting on the Eastern Front in December 1943. Clearly visible in the mid-section of the right mud guard are external air filter units (Filtzbalgvorschaltluftfilter), which were standard equipment until February 1944. [Bundesarchiv]

This skirtless Pz.Kpfw. IV Ausf. H was photographed somewhere on the Eastern Front in December 1943. [Bundesarchiv]

F2 vehicles in April 1942), as well as the vision port on the right side of the front plate. The driver's and radio operator's hatches were also modified. Beginning in June 1942 a stowage box was added on the left side of the hull for two spare road wheels. At the same time the roof of the turret lost the flare pistol port. In May 1943 a pre-filter assembly (Filzbalg-Vorschaltluftfilter) was added on the right mud guard. Consisting of two horizontal tubes the system provided preliminary filtering of the air entering the engine. Also around the same time the antenna mount was moved from the right side of the hull to the left side.

In March 1943 the last series of 700 tanks received spaced armor (Schürzen) which were designed to protect

Panzer grenadiers and their Pz.Kpfw. IV Ausf. H from an unidentified Wehrmacht unit operating on the Eastern Front in the first weeks of 1944. Clearly visible is the cylindrical exhaust stack mounted on the hull's rear wall. [Bundesarchiv]

Pz.Kpfw. IV Ausf. H from 1st Company of an unknown Wehrmacht tank regiment operating in Russia in early 1944. Tanks with missing or removed Schürzen plates were a common sight on the battlefield. [Bundesarchiv]

Pz.Kpfw. IV Ausf. H and German infantry from an unidentified Wehrmacht unit. Eastern Front, 1943/1944. The tank in the foreground was manufactured in the fall of 1943 as evidenced by all-steel return rollers and Zimmerit coating. [Bundesarchiv]

Pz.Kpfw. IV Ausf. H from an unknown unit operating on the Eastern Front in early 1944. [Bundesarchiv]

Pz.Kpfw. IV Ausf. H from an unknown Panzerwaffe unit photographed somewhere on the Eastern Front in early 1944. [Bundesarchiv]

the vehicles against anti-tank rifle fire and HEAT rounds. The skirts were 5 mm armor plates attached to a frame mounted on the tank's hull. The arrangement had an additional advantage of providing protection to the running gear. Similar armor was installed around the turret's side and rear walls. Turret-mounted Schürzen featured cut-outs placed over the standard access hatches. Hull-mounted skirts were removed for rail transport. Period photographs seem to prove that quite often only turret Schürzen were used.

In late 1942 the tanks operating in harsh winter conditions of the Eastern Front began to receive snow grousers, which increased the width of their tracks to 560 mm. In 1944 wider tracks went into service (so called Ostketten), which measured 568 mm in width. Both snow grousers and Ostketten were used in other variants of the tank as well.

TOWARDS A SIMPLIFIED DESIGN – PZ.KPFW. IV AUSF. H (SD.KFZ. 161/2)

The next iteration of the "IV" armed with the long 7,5 cm KwK 40 L/48 gun was designated Pz.Kpfw. IV Ausf. H (Sd. Kfz. 161/2). Nibelungwerke received an order for 2,500 examples of the vehicle, while Krupp and Vomag were each to deliver 1,400 tanks. Production began in May 1943 and in the end 2,322 tanks were delivered:

- Nibelungwerke: 1,250 vehicles, chassis numbers 85351-85750, 86601-87100 and 89101-89530;
- Vomag: 693 tanks, 84901-85350 and 86151-86393;
- Krupp: 379 examples, chassis numbers 84401 to 84791.

Some sources maintain that in fact 3,775 tanks were produced (84401-91500, or 84400-89540) out of a total order for 3,935 vehicles.

Pz.Kpfw. IV Ausf. F2 (G) "1233" from III./Pz.Rgt.24, 24th PzDiv., southern Russia, summer 1942.

Pz.Kpfw. IV Ausf. G "623" from II./Pz.Rgt.15, 11th PzDiv., Kursk, Russia, July 1943. The division fought at Kursk as part of Army Group South with only 25 long-barrelled Panzer IV tanks on strength. The vehicle wears two-tone color scheme: the sand base color (RAL 7028) is supplemented with thin green lines (RAL 6003), which were added after the tactical markings had been applied. Numerals and temporary Operation Zitadelle markings were black.

Painted by/Rysował: Jacek Pasieczny

inCOMBAT

Pz.Kpfw. IV Ausf. H "814" from II Battalion. 1st Pz.Reg., 1st PzDiv. Sandomierz beachhead, Poland, August 1944.

Pz.Kpfw. IV Ausf. H "1032" from Lt. Pilder's 10th Company, III Battalion, 24th Pz.Reg, 24th PzDiv. Poland, late summer 1944.

Painted by/Rysował: Arkadiusz Wrobel

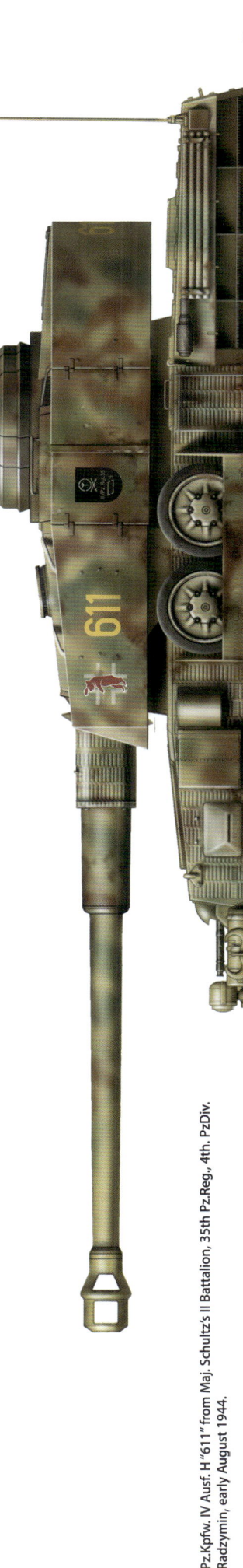

Pz.Kpfw. IV Ausf. H "224" from Obersturmführer Leopold Mittelbacher's 2nd Company, I Battalion, 5th SS Pz.Reg., 5th PzDiv. SS "Wiking", Warsaw area, September 1944.

Pz.Kpfw. IV Ausf. H "611" from Maj. Schultz's II Battalion, 35th Pz.Reg., 4th. PzDiv. Radzymin, early August 1944.

Painted by/Rysowat: ARKADIUSZ WRÓBEL

Pz.Kpfw. IV Ausf. H "600" belonged to the CO of 6th Company Lt. von Seyfried, II Battalion, 6th Pz.Reg., 3rd PzDiv. Sandomierz area, late August 1944.

Pz.Kpfw. IV Ausf. H "523" from II Battalion, 2nd Pz.Reg., 16th PzDiv. Sandomierz beachhead, early August 1944.

Painted by/Rysował: Arkadiusz Wrobel

Pz.Kpfw. IV Ausf. H "733" from Obersturmführer Mattern's 7th Company, II Battalion, 3rd SS Pz.Reg., 3rd SS PzDiv. SS "Totenkopf", Warsaw area, summer 1944.

Pz.Kpfw. IV Ausf. H "821" from Capt. Michaelis's II Battalion, 11th Pz.Reg., 6th PzDiv. Rozan, September 1944.

Painted by/Rysowal: ARKADIUSZ WROBEL

inCOMBAT

Pz.Kpfw. IV Ausf. H/J from l'Escadron Autonome de Chars Besnier, Saint-Nazaire, France, February – March 1945.

Pz.Kpfw. IV Ausf. J, 116th PzDiv., the Ardennes 1944.

Painted by/Rysował: Arkadiusz Wróbel

Pz.Kpfw. IV Ausf. J, 130th Pz.Reg., Pz.Lehr Div., Normandy 1944.

Pz.Kpfw. IV Ausf. J, 12th Pz.Div SS "Hitlerjugend", Germany 1944.

Painted by/Rysował: Arkadiusz Wrobel

Pz.Kpfw. IV Ausf. J, unknown unit, March 1945.

Pz.Kpfw. IV Ausf. J from 5. Samodzielny Dywizjon Artylerii Samochodowej, 6. Dywizja Piechoty, Poland, May 1945.

Painted by/Rysował: ARKADIUSZ WRÓBEL

inCOMBAT

Sheet/Arkusz 1

Rysował: Krzysztof Mucha

Pz.Kpfw. IV Ausf. J early production version. Hull of Ausf H with typical for it exhaust system, road wheel assemblies mounted using 4 bolts, one-piece hinged commander's hatch, 4 return rollers supporting tracks from Ausf H, metal frames/mounts for side skirts, different hubcaps on road wheels, light fan cover, new type of water valve intake for cooling system, Pilzen mounts for 2t crane (absent on vehicles produced prior to mid-June 1944), vehicle covered with Zimmerit paste.

Pz.Kpfw. IV Ausf. J pochodzący z bardzo wczesnej serii produkcyjnej. Wanna wersji H z typowym dla niej układem wydechowym, wózki jezdne mocowane do wanny na 4 śruby (chodzi o górny rząd śrub mocujących korpus wózka do bocznej ściany wanny), odchylana pokrywa wieżyczki dowódcy, 4 koła podtrzymujące gąsienice z wersji H, stelaże na ekrany chroniące wannę i kadłub wykonane z kątownika, ekrany płytowe, osłona wentylatora na wieży typu lekkiego, górna płyta wieży chroniona dodatkowymi ogniwami gąsienic, prawdopodobnie pojazd nie posiadał „grzybków" (Pilzen) do mocowania dźwigu 2t tak jak wszystkie pojazdy montowane do połowy czerwca 1944 r., ogniwa gąsienic pochodzące z wersji G/H, kadłub pokryty pastą Zimmerit.

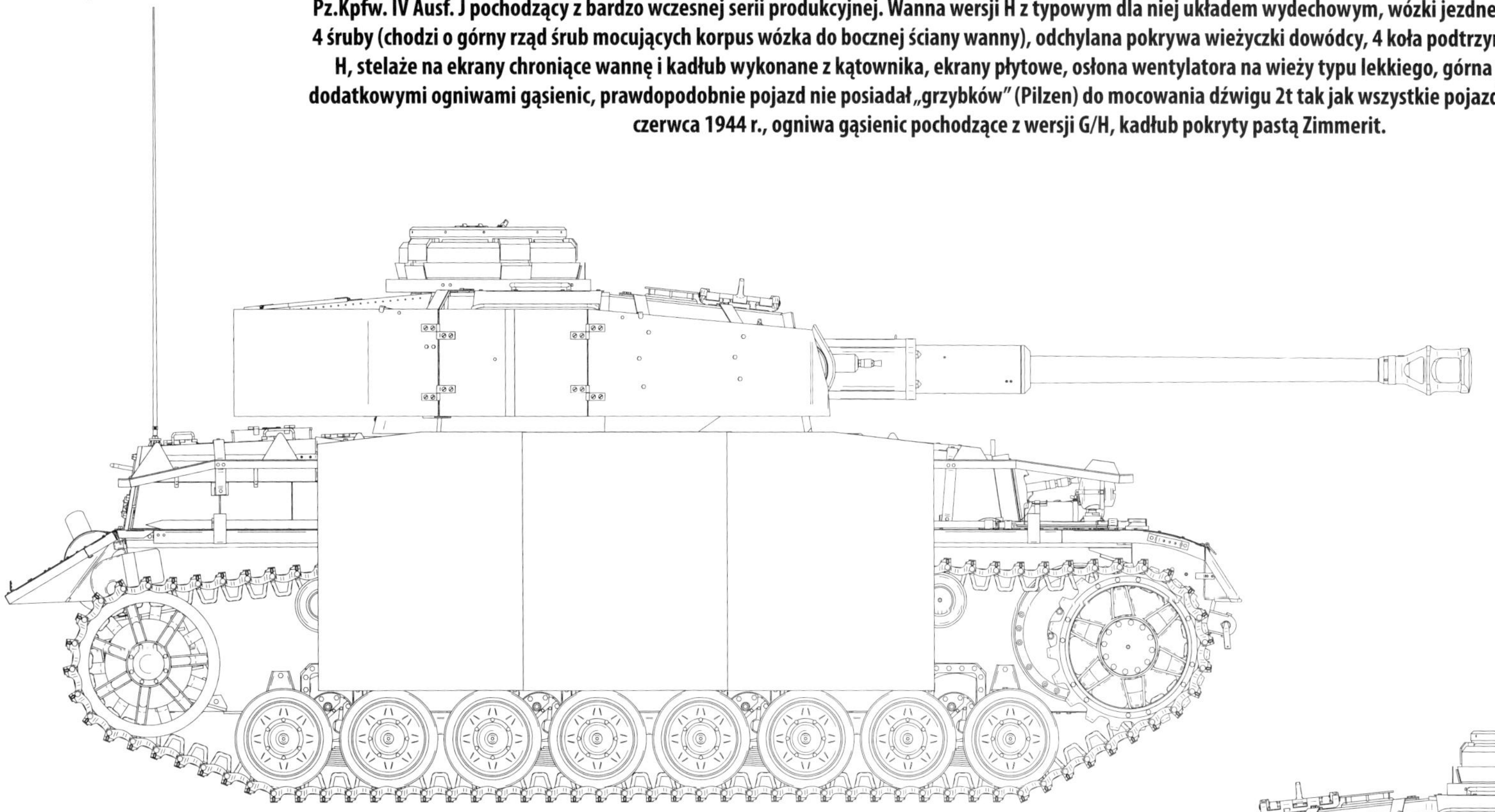

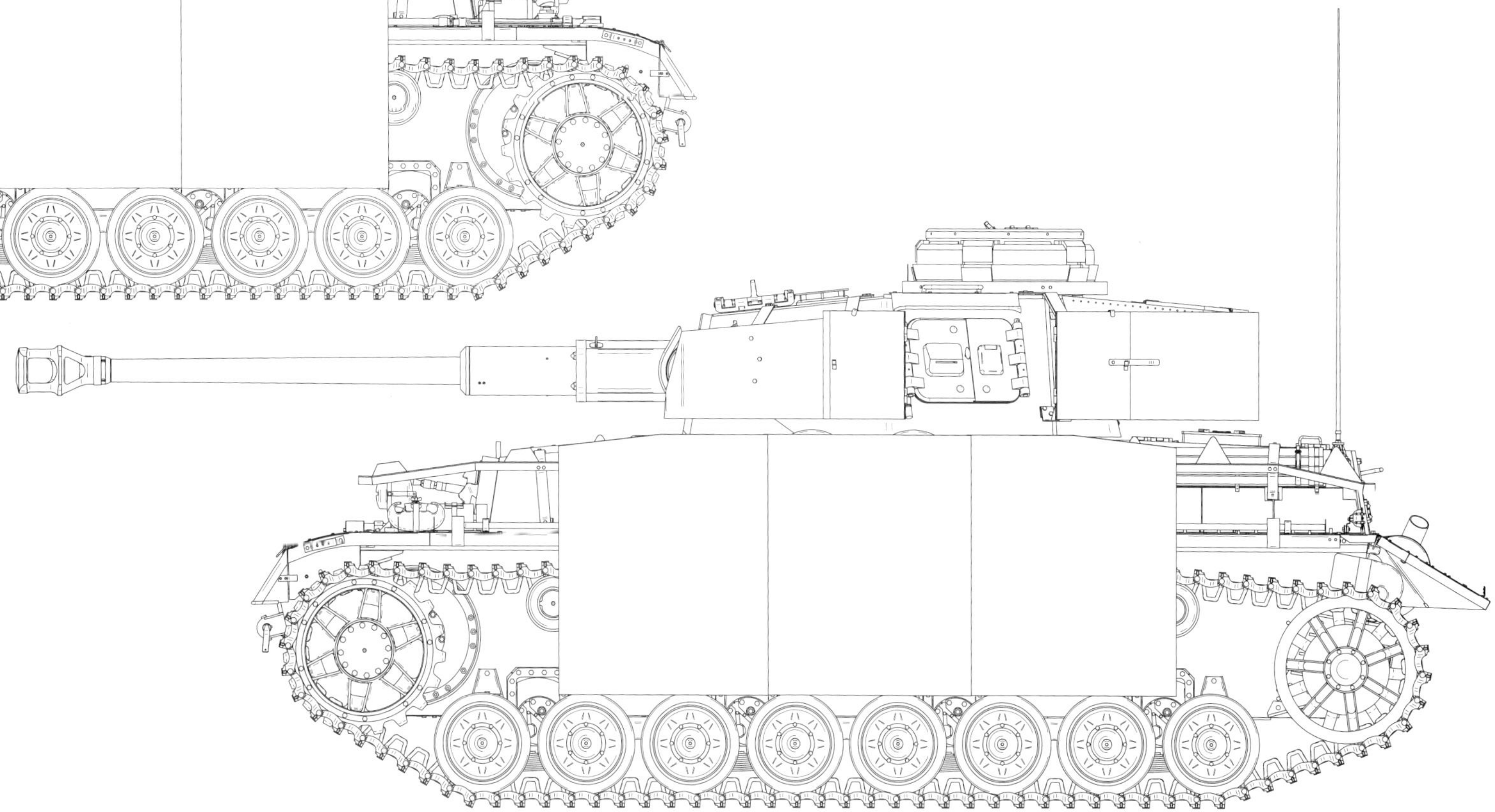

Scale/skala: 1/35

www.kagero.eu
www.shop.kagero.pl

inCOMBAT

Sheet/Arkusz 2

Rysował: Krzysztof Mucha

Pz.Kpfw. IV Ausf. J late production version. Modified hull with „handles" and 4 return rollers, strengthened hull „handles" (!), road wheel assemblies mounted using 4 bolts, mount for 10 extra track link on the front hull plate, lack of metal frames/mounts for side skirts, sides and front hull protected by extra track links, commander's cupola with rotating hatch, front turret protected by extra track links.

Pz.Kpfw. IV Ausf. J pochodzący z początku ostatniej serii produkcyjnej. Zmodyfikowane boki wanny z „uszami", przednia płyta wanny z uchwytami holowniczymi (!), 4 koła podtrzymujące gąsienice z wersji H, wózki jezdne mocowane na 4 śruby, na przedniej płycie wanny 10 dodatkowych ogniw gąsienic, brak stelaży na ekrany chroniące wannę i kadłub, boki i przód kadłuba chroniony dodatkowymi ogniwami gąsienic, pokrywa wieżyczki dowódcy na sworzniu obrotowym, przód wieży chroniony dodatkowymi ogniwami gąsienic.

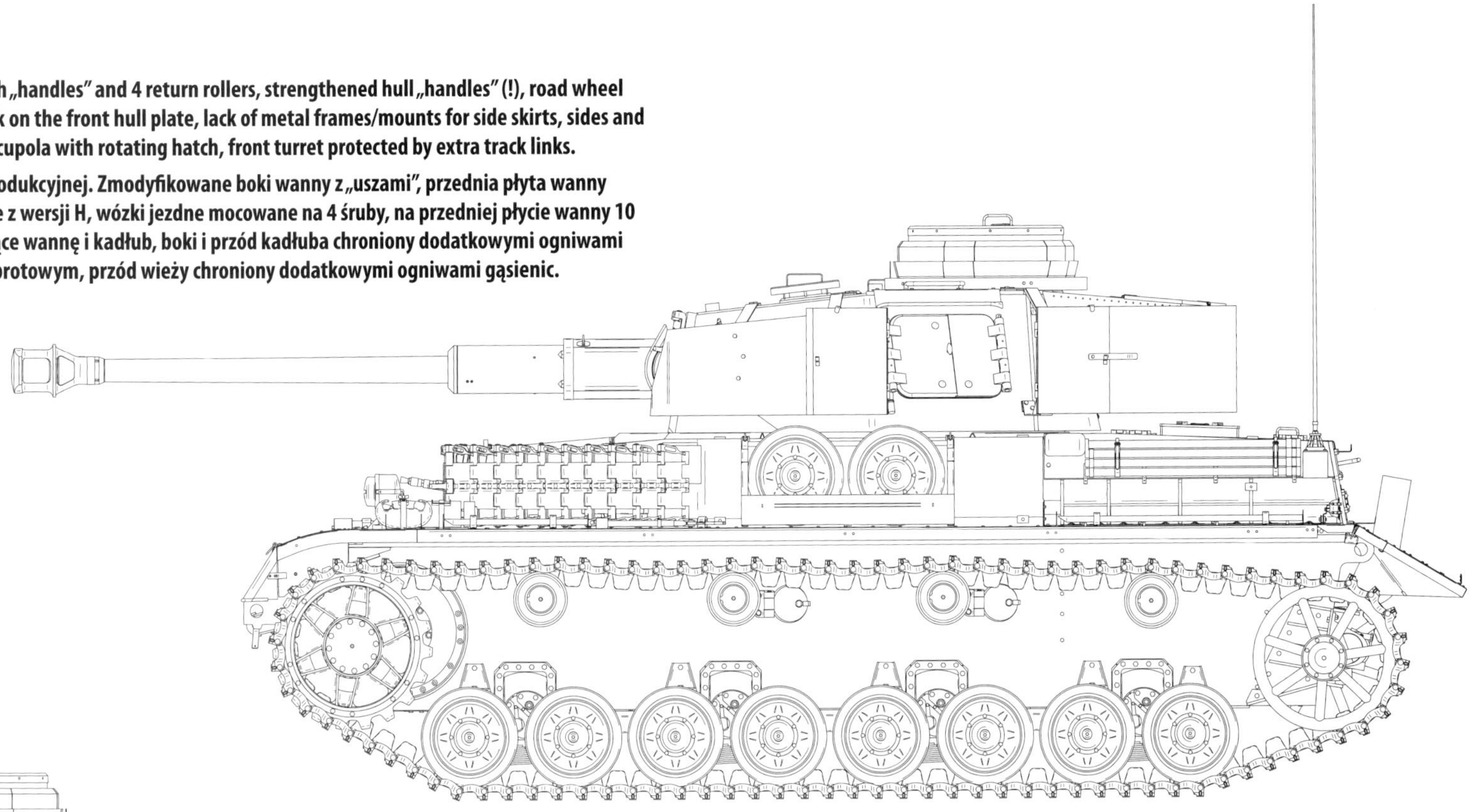

Scale/skala: 1/35

www.kagero.eu
www.shop.kagero.pl

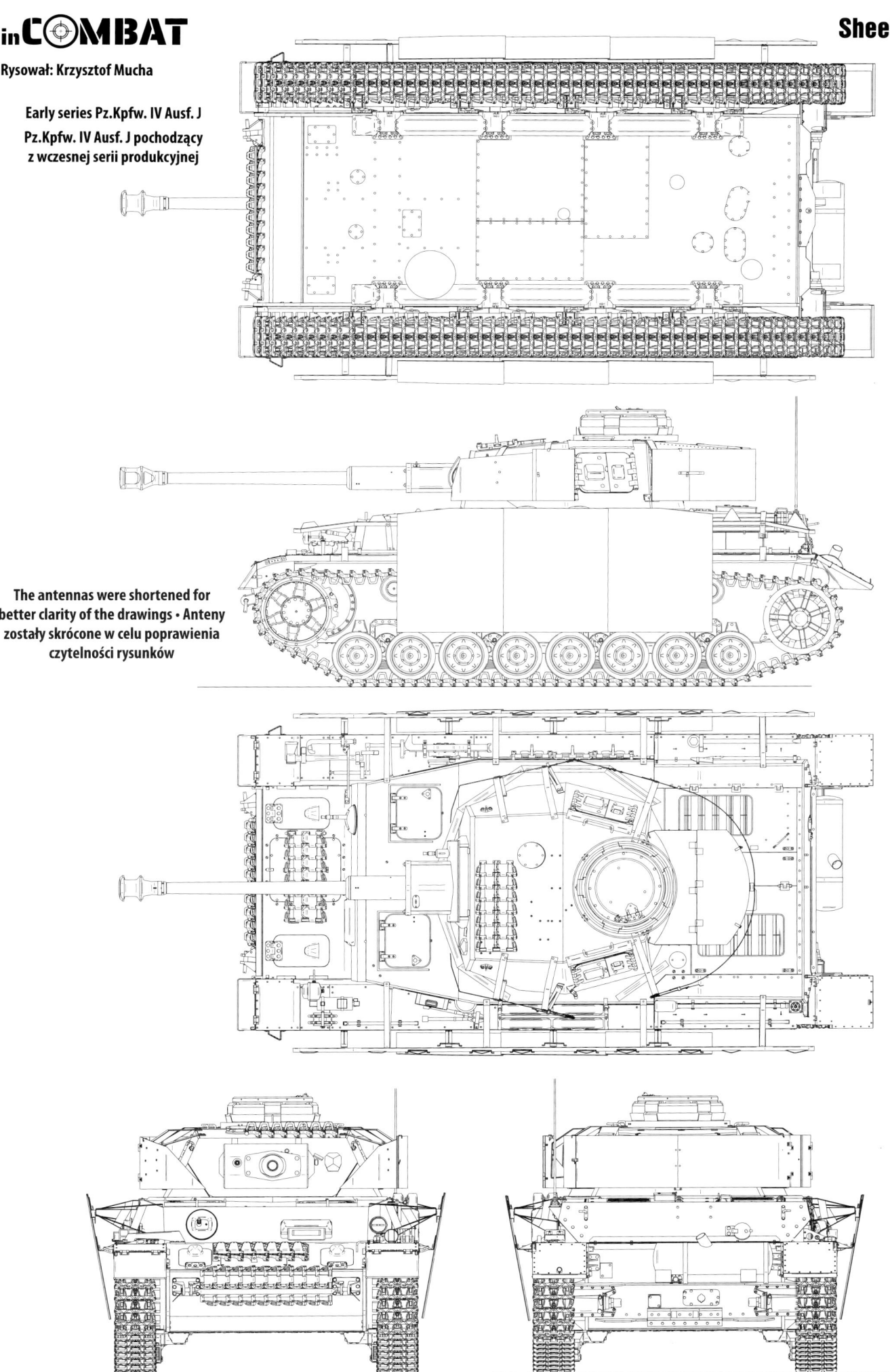

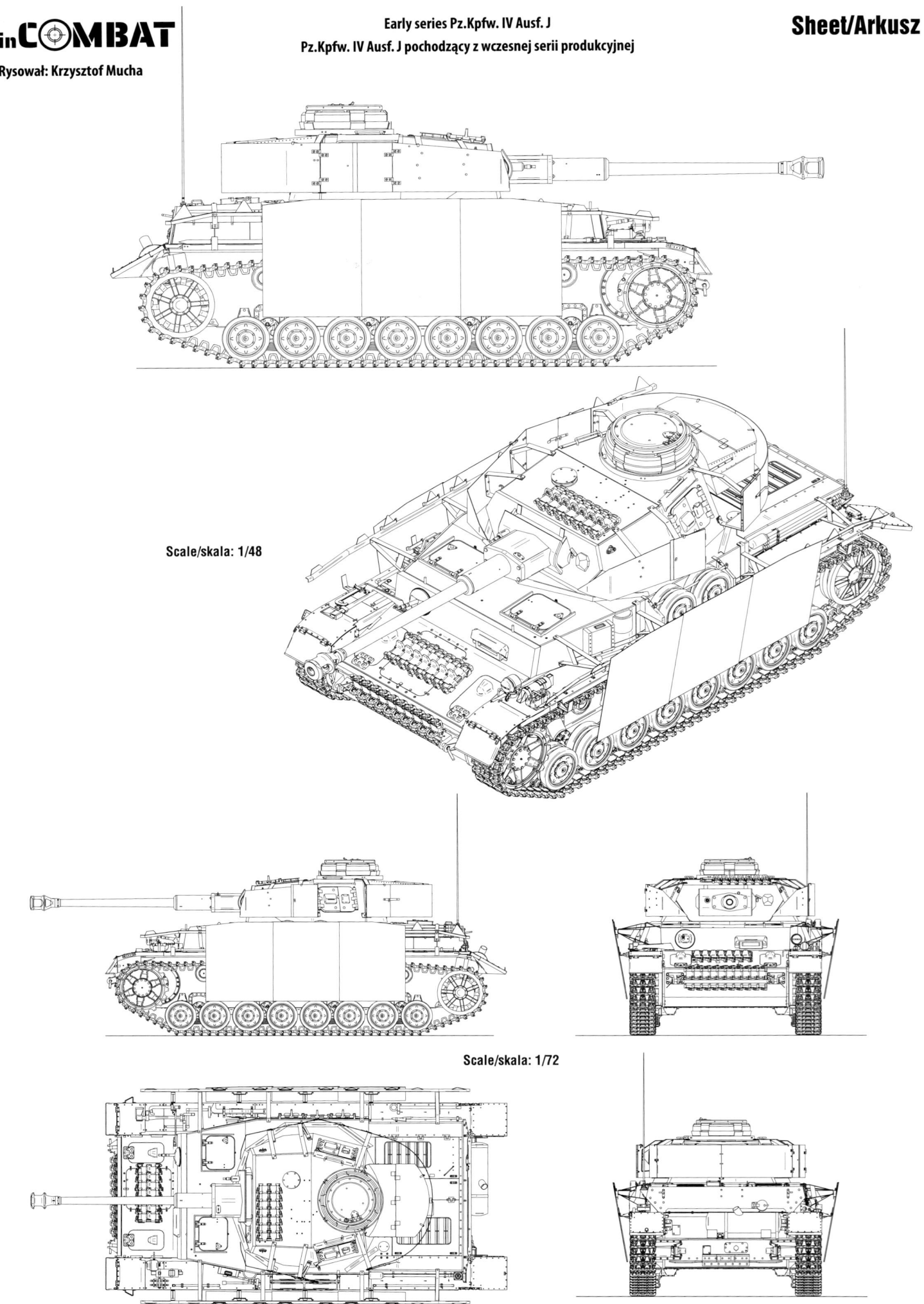

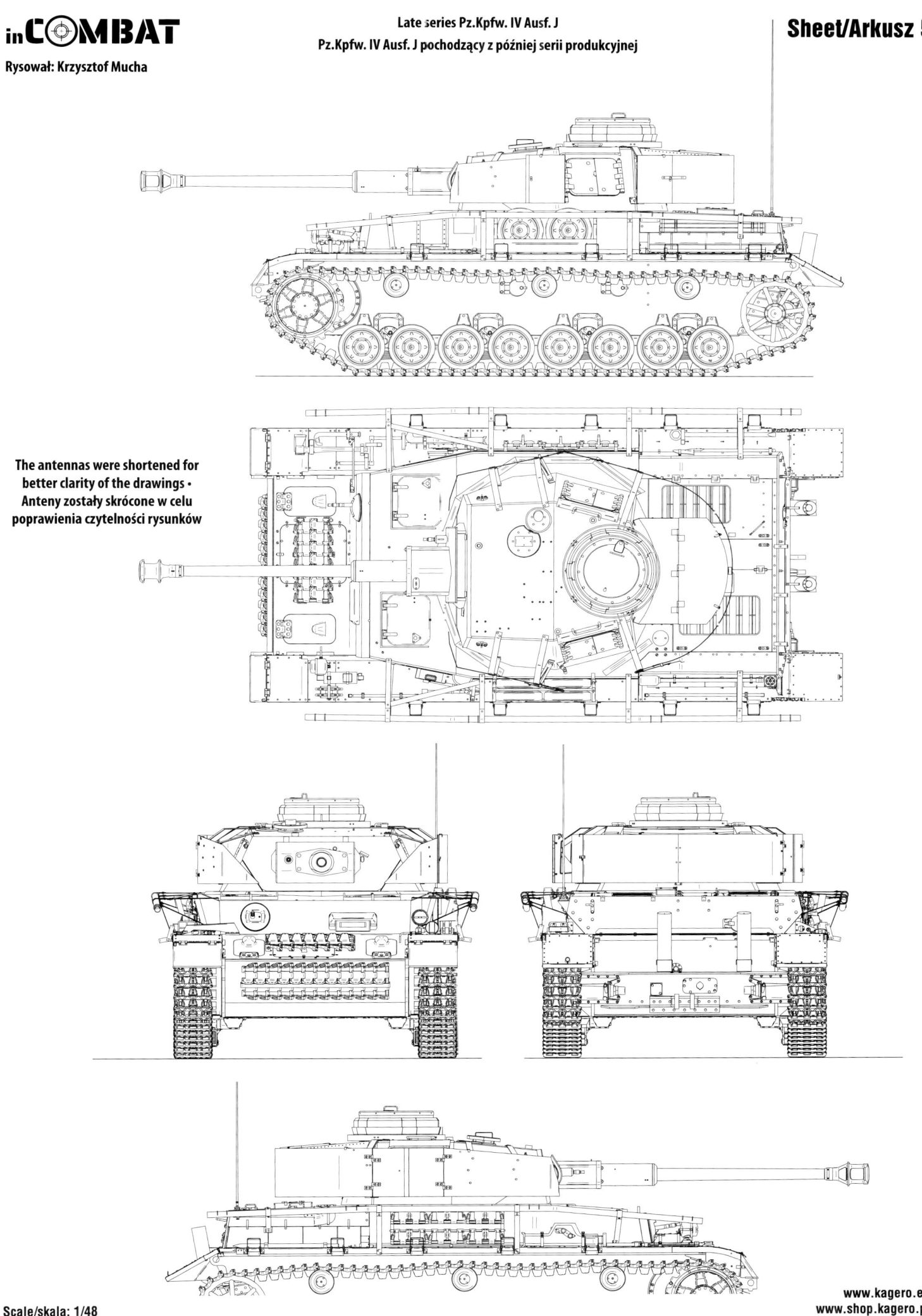

Late series Pz.Beob.Wg. IV Ausf. J
Pz.Bef.Wg. IV Ausf. J pochodzący z późniejszej serii produkcyjnej

Sheet/Arkusz 6

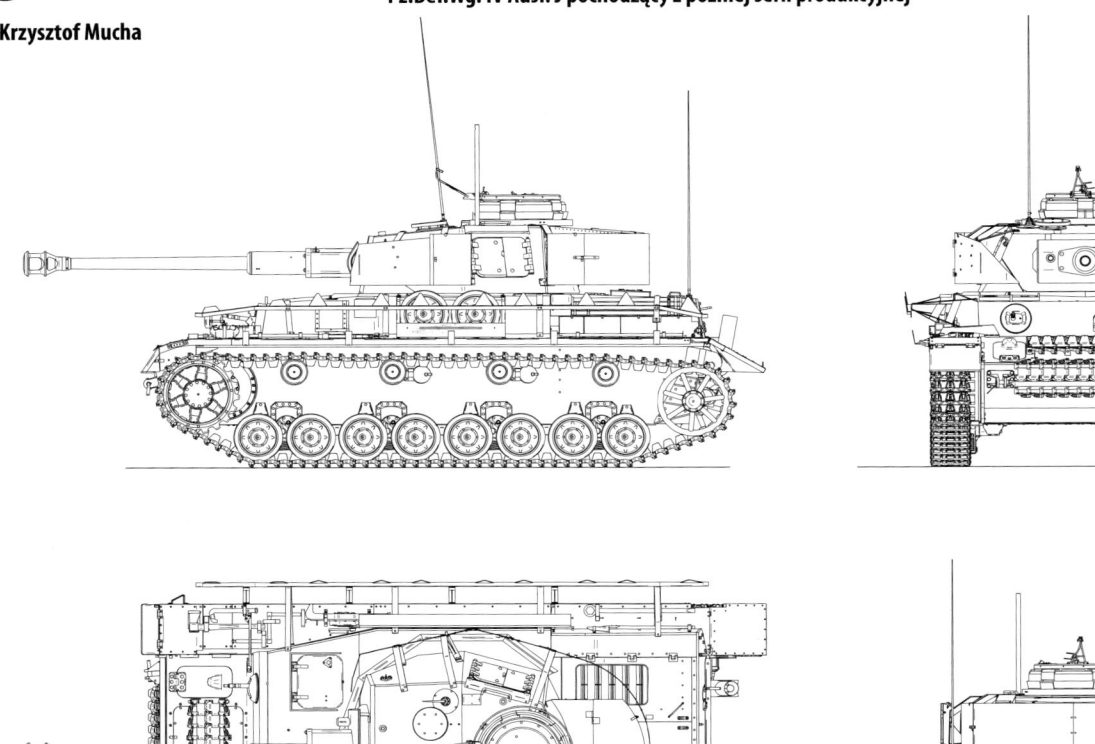

Late series Pz.Beob.Wg. IV Ausf. J
Pz.Beob.Wg. IV Ausf. J pochodzący z późniejszej serii produkcyjnej

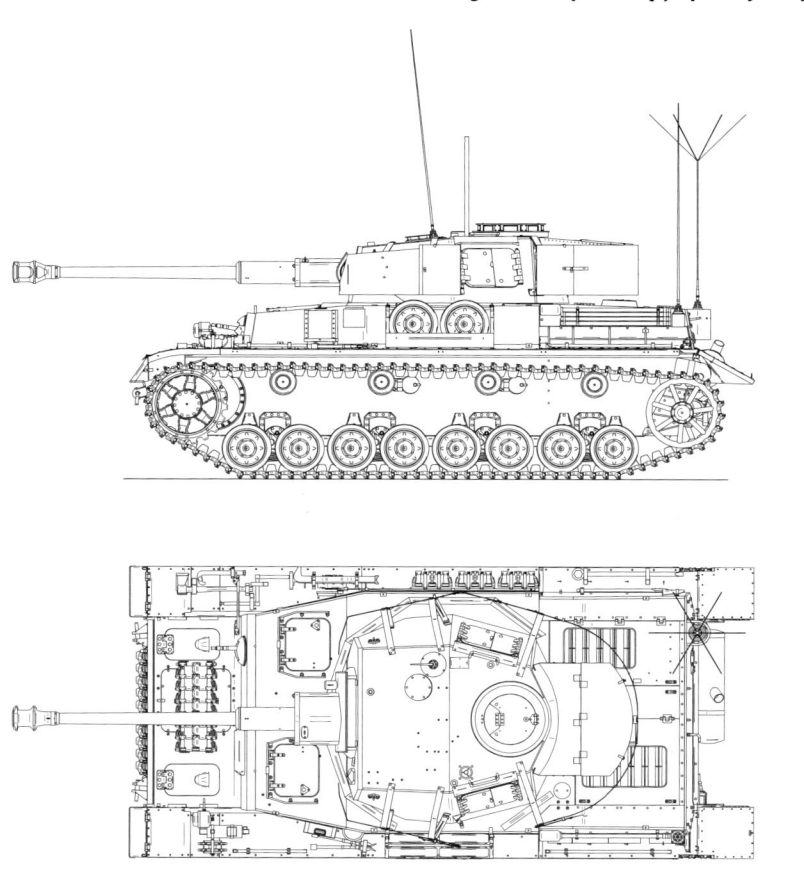
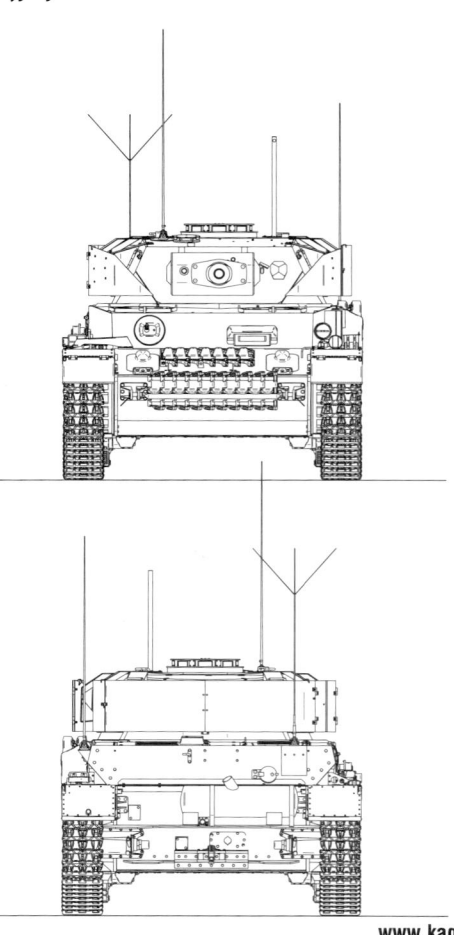

Scale/skala: 1/72

www.kagero.eu
www.shop.kagero.pl

Zahnradfabrik ZF Aphon SSG 77 transmission which was used in Pz.Kpfw. IV Ausf. H and Ausf. J. The same unit was installed in earlier Pz.Kpfw. III vehicles. [3D render: Samir Karmieh]

The design of Ausf. H and, later, Ausf J models clearly show a drive to gradually simplify the tank's design. This was due mainly to the pressure to speed up the production of the vehicles, but also due to shortages of certain materials. Not counting armament, optics or radio gear, a single Pz.Lpfw. IV required 39,000 kg of steel, 1.2 kg of tin, 195.1 kg of copper, 238 kg of aluminum, 63.3 kg of lead, 66.4 kg of zinc, 0.15 kg of magnesium and 116.3 kg of potassium.

One of the main differences compared to the earlier versions was the redesigned running gear introduced in September 1943. The design included simplified drive wheels, cast idlers replacing earlier welded tube wheels and all-steel return rollers. Road wheels received simplified armored hubcaps. The tanks rolling off production lines from June 1943 onwards received thicker armor. Initially a 30 mm armor plate was added to the main armor, which was then replaced with an 80 mm plate. The turret's roof also received thicker armor protection. The tanks armor was as follows:
- front superstructure – 80 mm, sloped at 9° to vertical;
- glacis: 20 mm, sloped at 70°;
- hull mid front plate: 80 mm, 12°;
- hull lower plate: 30 mm, 60°;
- sides: 30 mm (0°) and 20 mm (rear part sloped at 10°);
- rear deck: 20 mm, 10°;
- rear lower hull plate: 14.5 mm, 74°;
- roof: 10 – 11 mm, 85 – 90°;
- bottom: 10 mm, 90°.

Turret's armor protection was as follows:
- front plate: 50 mm sloped at 10° to vertical;
- curved mantlet plate: 50 mm;
- sides: 30 mm, 25°;
- curved rear plate: 30 mm, 16° to 26°;
- roof: 16 mm, 84° in the front section and 90° I the rear.

From the very beginning of the production run the tanks were equipped with spaced armor (Schürzen). Additional armor protection drove the vehicle's weight up to 25 tons, which in turn degraded its performance. The tank was slower than its predecessors with top speed around 38 km/h.

In January 1944 a roof-mounted grenade launcher was introduced (Nahverteidigungswaffe). Later, towards the end of the production run in February 1944, the Filzbalg-Vorschaltluftfilter air filtering system was dropped. The reason was dirt accumulating between the main armor and armored skirts, which, in the worst case scenario, led to the clogging of filter canisters. In June gun ports in the rear plate of the turret were eliminated, as were vision ports in superstructure sides, oval openings in driver's and radio operator's hatch covers used flare gun ports. Most of those openings were in fact redundant once the armored skirts had been introduced, because they blocked the view anyway. In addition, they did little to improve the armor's strength. There were more modifications introduced to the design. Commander's cupola received a leather cushion underneath the cover and a special protective ring at its base. The base of the cupola

Maybach 120 TRM engine powered Pz.Kpfw. IV Ausf. F2/G-J tanks. [3D render: Samir Karmieh]

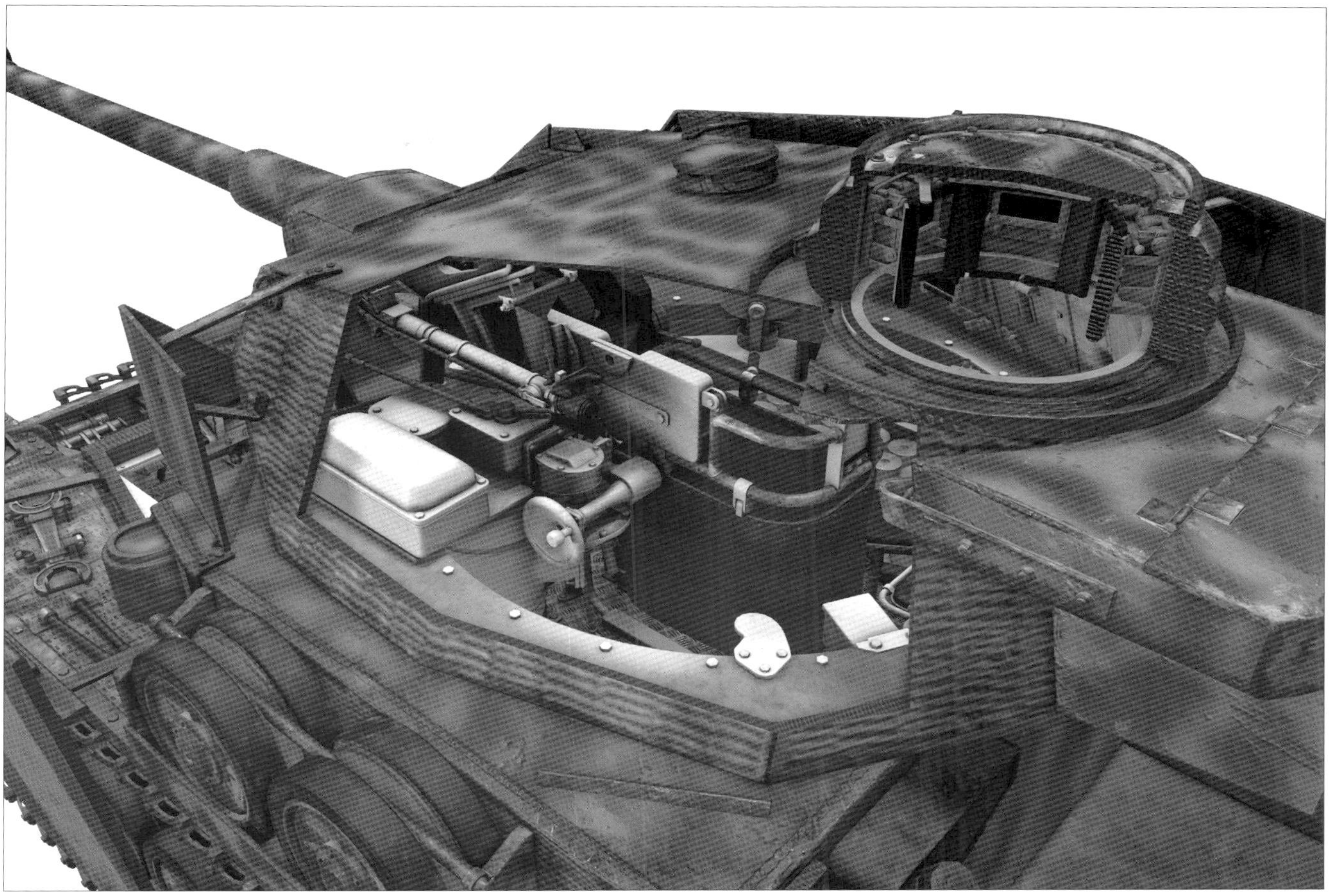

A cross section of the turret of the Pz.Kpfw. IV Ausf. H. Details of the commander's cupola and 75 mm gun are clearly visible. [3D render: Samir Karmieh]

saw the introduction of a mount for the 41 or 42 anti-aircraft machine gun.

The tank also received a six-speed Zahnradfabrik ZF SGG 77 transmission. Speeds at different gears were as follows:
- 1 – 4.2 km/h;
- 2 – 8.1 km/h;
- 3 – 13.8 km/h;
- 4 – 20.8 km/h;
- 5 – 29.5 km/k;
- 6 – 38 km/h;
- reverse – 5.2 km/h.

In 1943 Panzerwaffe began to apply Zimmerit coating to its combat vehicles – a special ceramic paste with antimagnetic properties, designed to protect the hulls from magnetic mines. Zimmerit was supplied by Chemische Werke Zimmer from Berlin. The paste was composed of polyvinyl acetate (commonly used as wood glue) – 25 percent, sawdust – 10 percent, barium sulfate – 40 percent, zinc sulfide – 10 percent and pigment (ochre) – 15 percent.

Per factory instructions Zimmerit was to be applied to vertical armored surfaces, but in the field it was liberally used on every surface that enemy infantry could possibly access, including horizontal surfaces and spaced armor. Zimmerit had a consistency of a thick paste or putty. Before the application of Zimmerit the vehicle usually received a coat of anti-corrosive paint, but that wasn't a requirement. Typically, Zimmerit was applied in two layers. The first one was about 5 mm thick and shaped into a patchwork of rectangles. Jagged edges of the squares mad it easier for the second layer to stick. The latter served as the actual protection against magnetic mines, but also offered a degree of camouflage. The outer layer was thinner than the first one and created a wavy pattern on the tank's armor. On average it took about 24 hours for the paste to set, but the process could be shortened to around two hours by heating the treated surfaces with a special soldering iron.

In April 1944 Zimmerit coating was dropped, for a number of reasons. First, rumors circulated among the crews that the paste was combustible, although this wasn't confirmed by tests. Another reason was rapid developments of Allied anti-tank weapons against which Zimmerit offered no protection. There was also the weight issue – a coating of Zimmerit increased the vehicle's weight by some 100 kg. Finally, even the time it took to apply the paste mattered when German factories, under a constant threat of air attacks, struggled to maintain a steady flow of new tanks for frontline units.

Zimmerit's usefulness as a protect on against magnetic mines has also been questioned. However, it certainly offered a degree of camouflage as its rough and matt surface absorbed light making tanks more difficult to detect.

FINAL VERSION – PZ.KPFW. IV AUSF. J (SD.KFZ. 161/2)

Production of the final iteration of the tank, designated Pz.Kpfw. IV Ausf. J (10 Serie/B.W.) Sd.Kfz. 161/2, began in February 1944. By April 1945 Nibelungwerke plant delivered 2,980 vehicles (chassis numbers 89531-90600, 91300-93250 and 110001-1104150, while Vomag produced 180 tanks (86394-86573) for a total of 3,160 machines. Krupp, which until then had been heavily involved in the production of the

A cross section of the turret of the Pz.Kpfw. IV Ausf. H/J. Shown to a good advantage are details of the 7,5 cm KwK 40 L/48 gun and canvas bag for spent casings hung under the breech. [3D render: Samir Karmieh]

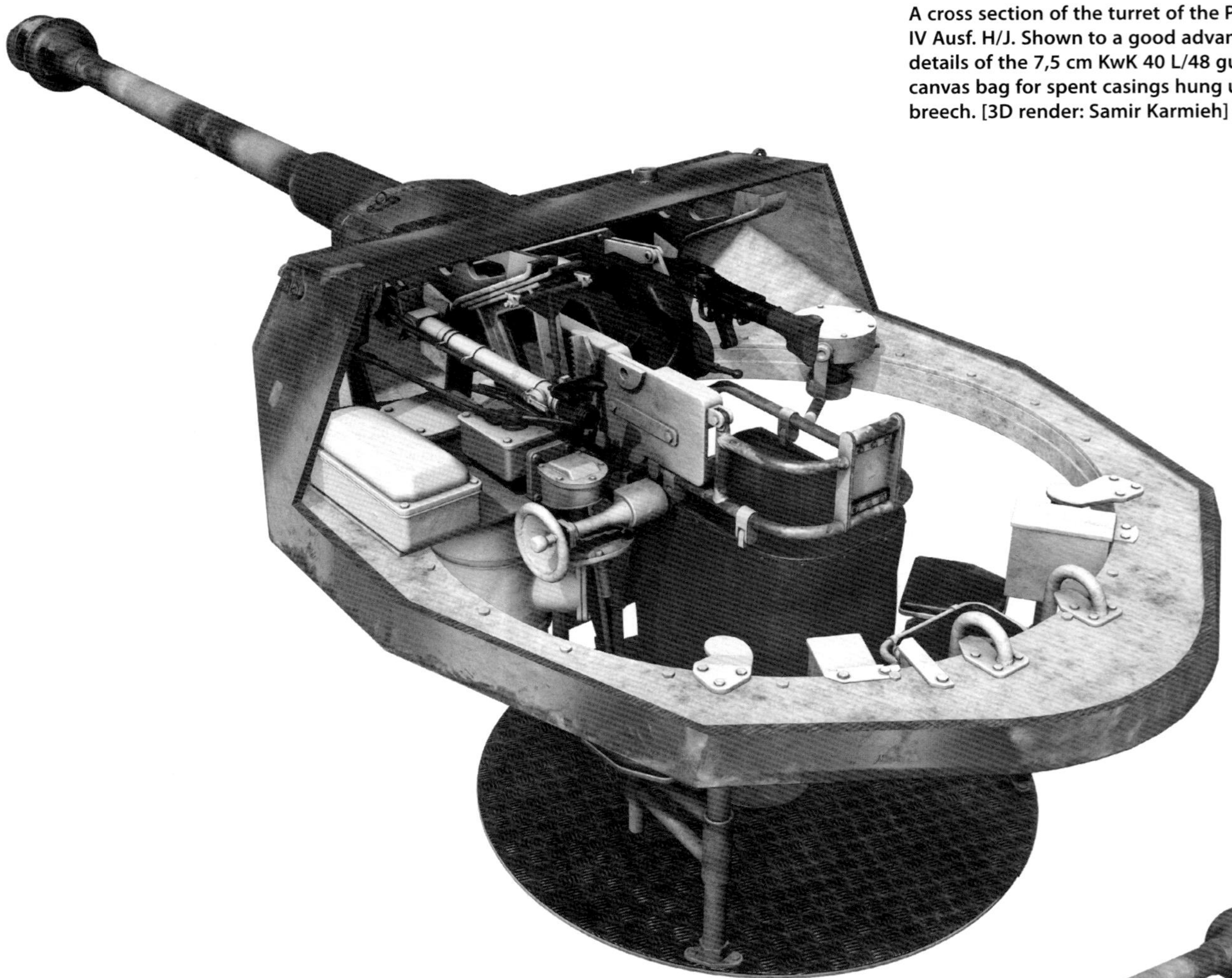

This Pz.Kpfw. IV Ausf. H from 27tj Tank Regiment (19th PzDiv.) was destroyed near Kuznica on July 23, 1944. Notice the lack of external stowage box behind the turret and all-steel return rollers. [Robert Wróblewski's collection]

A well-camouflaged Pz.Kpfw. IV Ausf. H from I Battalion, 35th Tank Regiment (4th PzDiv.) photographed on the Eastern Front in the summer of 1944. The unit's insignia – a stylized rendition of a bear – can be seen on the turret's spaced armor. [Robert Wróblewski's collection]

"IV", switched to manufacturing of Sturmgeschütz IV assault guns. At the same time Vomag launched production of Jagdpanzer IV tank destroyers. Some sources claim that the number of vehicles produced was anywhere from 1,758 to 2,393 examples (chassis numbers from 91501 to unknown, or from 86394 to 97000).

The design of the Ausf. J model showed further simplification to allow a more rapid production rate. In June 1944 the DKW 500 engine driving the turret traverse mechanism was dropped from the design. From then on the turret could only be traversed manually at a rate of 12.5° in four seconds. In place of the engine the tank received an additional 210 l fuel tank, which brought the total fuel capacity to 680 l. The tank's range also increased to 210 km in cross-country conditions or 320 km on roads. In hindsight those changes made little sense since they were introduced in late stages of the war when the Reich was already struggling to maintain a steady flow of propellants. The new fuel tank was therefore nothing more than a useless addition to fill the space where the DKW 500 engine used to be. To make things even worse, the new tanks were notoriously leaky, which created a fire hazard. For that reason the tanks were not installed in early production examples of the Ausf. J.

This Pz.Kpfw. IV Ausf. H belonged to the CO, 6th Company, II Battalion, 6th Tank Regiment (3rd PzDiv.). The photograph was taken during fighting in Sandomierz area in August 1944. [Robert Wróblewski's collection]

These three Pz.Kpfw. IV Ausf. H tanks from 8th Company, II Battalion, 6th Tank Regiment (3rd PzDiv.) where most likely photographed during training in Poland in the summer of 1944. [Robert Wróblewski's collection]

Pz.Kpfw. IV Ausf. H from II Platoon, 6th Company, II Battalion, 6th Tank Regiment (3rd PzDiv.) in Sandomierz area, Poland. August 1944. [Robert Wróblewski's collection]

A series of photographs of Pz.Kpfw. IV Ausf. H tank from II Platoon, 6th Company, II Battalion, 6th Tank Regiment (3rd PzDiv.) commanded by Lt. vor Korff. The vehicle is equipped with Schürzen spaced armor only on the right hand side. Sandomierz beachhead, August 1944. [Robert Wróblewski's collection]

Pz.Kpfw. IV Ausf. H from 6th Company, II Battalion, 130th Tank Regiment (Panzer-Lehr Div.) destroyed by the British during fighting at Villers-Bocage on June 13, 1944. [Bundesarchiv]

From the very beginning of the production run the new model was equipped with spaced armor, but in 1944/45 solid plates were replaced with Drahtgeflechtschürzen (also known as Thoma Schürzen) – wire mesh screens mounted on a frame. Those were not only twenty percent lighter than the standard skirts, but also required a lot less metal to manufacture. In addition, the screens offered more flexibility in camouflage and reduced dirt build-up normally accumulating between spaced armor and running gear.

In June 1944 some of the vehicles received turret-mounted brackets (so called Pilzen) for a collapsible two-ton crane. In July the armored protection of the turret increased to 18 mm on the roof and 26 mm in the rear. A smoke grenade launcher was also added to the turret's roof. In November vision ports on turret's hatch covers were removed, as were gun ports in the turret's rear plate. Both were redundant since the installation of armored skirts made observation or firing from those ports impossible. At the same time the radio operator's access hatch was moved back. Some of the tanks didn't have a vision port in the turret's front plate.

The tank's exhaust system underwent significant changes as well. While early Ausf. J models still had the original version of the system, those manufactured from August onwards featured two vertical exhaust pipes known as Flammenvernichter or Flammentöter. In October towing hooks were replaced with simplified towing hold cut in the extended side armor plate. In addition, the commander's cupola was redesigned to include a swivel hatch cover, opening upwards and rotating to the right. The running gear also underwent modifications. All-steel return rollers were introduced, which were reduced in number from four to three in all vehicles produced after December 1944. The design of road wheels was also further simplified. From September 1944 factories stopped applying Zimmerit to newly produced tanks.

It is perhaps worth noting that parts cannibalized from various versions of the tank were often installed in vehicles undergoing overhauls, which is perhaps why there is such an abundance of non-standard machines appearing in period photographs. Accurate identification of late production versions of the tank is further complicated by the fact that the vehicles were almost continuously modified, both on the assembly lines and in the field.

ORGANIZATION OF PANZER UNITS AND BRIEF COMBAT HISTORY

On the eve of invasion of Poland in September 1939 German forces had seven armored divisions (1st, 2nd, 3rd, 4th, 5th, 10th PzDiv. and PzDiv. "Kempf"), as well as four light divisions (1st, 2nd, 3rd and 4th Leichte Division). The latter didn't

Pz.Kpfw. IV Ausf. J from 3rd SS Tank Regiment (3rd PzDiv. SS "Totenkopf"). Eastern Front, summer 1944. [Bundesarchiv]

This photograph of early production Pz.Kpfw. IV Ausf. J tank was most likely taken in Poland in the summer of 1944. The vehicle belonged to II Platoon, 5th Company, II Battalion 3rd SS Tank Regiment (3rd PzDiv. SS "Totenkopf"). [Robert Wróblewski's collection]

Repairs are being carried out of the final drive of this Pz.Kpfw. IV Ausf. H or Ausf. J from an unidentified tank regiment. Eastern Front, summer 1944. [Bundesarchiv]

These early production Pz.Kpfw. IV Ausf. J examples belonged to 2nd SS Tank Regiment (2nd PzDiv. SS "Das Reich") were destroyed in Normandy in 1944. [Kagero archives]

A German armored column destroyed by Allied aircraft on the Western Front in the summer of 1944. The vehicle in the middle is an early production Pz.Kpfw. IV Ausf. H or Pz.Kpfw. IV Ausf. J. [Kagero archives]

Early production Pz.Kpfw. IV Ausf. J from an unidentified unit, 1944. [Kagero archives]

live up to expectations and by the time Germany launched an invasion of France, Belgium, Holland and Luxembourg those units were reformed as 6th, 7th, 8th and 9th PzDiv., raising the total number of German armored division to ten. At the same time the provisional Panzer Division "Kempf" was deactivated.

While the western campaign was still going on, German planners were busy working on a new armored forces development strategy. The plan was to establish ten new panzer divisions (11th – 20th), but a severe shortage of combat vehicles meant that even the existing units could barely maintain

Pz.Kpfw. IV Ausf. J from 24th Tank Regiment, 24th PzDiv. knocked out during fighting in East Prussia in early 1945. Note three all-steel return rollers – a characteristic feature of the final production version of the "IV". [Kagero archives]

Pz.Kpfw. IV Ausf. J from 5th Company, II Battalion, 31st Tank Regiment (5th PzDiv.) lost in combat in East Prussia, winter 1944/45. Note the regimental insignia – the devil's head – painted on the turret. [Kagero archives]

adequate strength. In order to increase the number of available armored divisions the existing units had to be re-organized by reducing the number of armored regiments in each division from two to just one. This generated "savings", which could then be allocated to newly formed divisions. Each new unit consisted of a single armored regiment split into two bat-talions. As a result, while the number of panzer units actually increased, the numbers of armored vehicles fielded by those units dropped.

Production of first long-barreled Pz.Kpfw. IVs began in May 1942. At the time German panzer divisions were still organized based on the 1941 structure. A typical tank regiment

Pz.Kpfw. IV Ausf. H from 6th Company, II Battalion, 1st SS Tank Regiment (1st PzDiv. SS "Leibstandarte Adolf Hitler") parked in front of the Nativity of St. Mary Cathedral in Milan, September 1943. The tank is equipped with Zusatzpanzerung. [Bundesarchiv]

(Panzerregiment) was organized as follows, based on the official organizational tables (Kriegsstärke Nachweisung – K.St.N.) from November 1, 1941:
- regimental HQ - Stab Panzerregiment, K.St.N. 1103,
- tank battalion HQ (two battalions per regiment) – Stab Panzrabteilung, K.St.N. 1107,
- tank battalion HQ company – Stabskompanie Panzerabteilung, K.St.N. 1150
- light tank company (two companies per battalion) – leichte Panzerkompanie, K.St.N. 1171,
- medium tank company – mittlere Panzerkompanie, K.St.N. 1175,
- reserve section - Staffel Panzerabteilung, K.St.N. 1178.

In those days the role of combating enemy armor was assigned to Pz.Kpfw. IIIs, hence the "IVs", tasked with combat support, were much less common in armored divisions.

Early production example of the Pz.Kpfw. IV Ausf. H from 9th Company, 3rd SS Tank Regiment (3rd Pz.Gren.Div. SS "Totenkopf") in Kursk area, early July 1943. Division's tactical markings used during operation Zitadelle are applied to front armor plate. [Bundesarchiv]

Due to constant problems with a steady supply of combat vehicles panzer divisions were never fully standardized in terms of strength and equipment mix. Therefore regiments often differed in their organizational structure – some might have two tank battalions on strength, while others only two, which translated into a varying number of tanks in service. Some regiments had over 40 Panzer IV tanks on strength.

Further reorganization of panzer divisions took place between 1942 and 1945. Changes were also introduced at the tank regiment level, which now included two tank battalions as standard. Furthermore, lessons learned in combat showed beyond doubt that a large number of light tanks was no longer a viable concept, while Pz.Kpfw. III, even armed with 50 and 75 mm guns, were no longer a formidable force they used to be. Their place took new Pz.Kpfw. V "Panther" medium tanks, which, along with the long-barreled "IVs", became the core fighting force of a tank regiment. One of the regiment's battalions was typically equipped with "Panthers", while the other used Pz.Kpfw. IVs. In 1943 a tank regiment organizational structure was as follows:

- regimental HQ - Stab Panzerregiment, K.St.N. 1103,
- tank battalion HQ (two battalions per regiment) – Stab Panzrabteilung, K.St.N. 1107
- tank battalion HQ company – Stabskompanie Panzerabteilung, K.St.N. 1150b,
- flame thrower tank platoon – Panzerflammzug (only in selected panzer divisions), K.St.N. 1190
- four medium tank companies –mittlere Panzerkompanie, K.St.N. 1175a.

Therefore each battalion was supposed to have five Panzer IV tanks in HQ reconnaissance platoon and two vehicles of the type in HQ of each of the four companies, plus 20 machines in each company (split into four platoons) for a total of 93 tanks. In some cases however some of the Pz.Kpfw. IVs were replaced with less capable "IIIs".

For a limited period of time Panzer IVs were also assigned to independent armored brigades. The first ten such brigades (101st to 110th) were formed in July 1944, but those were supposed to be equipped with Pz.Kpfw. V "Panther" tanks. Three more brigades were established in September that year (111th to 113th) with Pz.Kpfw. IVs on strength. Those were assigned to three companies of 14 vehicles each, which formed a tank battalion. The second battalion was equipped with "Panther" tanks. The brigades didn't last very long and were deactivated later in the fall. Their tanks were distributed among the existing panzer divisions: vehicles from the 111th Brigade were assigned to 11th Panzer Division, tanks from the 112th Brigade went to 21st Panzer Division, while those on strength of 113th Brigade ended up with 15th Panzergrenadier Division.

Another modification of the panzer division structure was introduced in 1945. Now each panzer division was to include a single tank regiment consisting of a tank battalion and a tank grenadier battalion. The tank battalion was to include four tank companies, each equipped with 40 vehicles – two with Pz.Kpfw. Vs and two with Panzer IVs.

Based on organizational tables Pz.Kpfw. IVs were on strength of medium tank companies within a panzer battalion, each equipped with 14 vehicles (two in company HQ section and four in each of the three platoons). Additionally, each company had a light tank platoon (five vehicles) equipped with Pz.Kpfw. IIs. A single "IV" was also assigned to the reserve section. In total, a standard tank regiment had 29 Pz.Kpfw. IVs on strength.

Early production Pz.Kpfw. IV Ausf. H and Pz.Kpfw. IV Ausf. G (in the background) from 9. Company, 3rd SS Tank Regiment (3rd Pz.Gren.Div. SS "Totenkopf"). Kursk area, early July 1943. [Bundesarchiv]

First examples of the Pz.Kpfw. IV Ausf. F2 went into service in May 1942 and were soon deployed to North Africa, where they took part in fighting at Bir Hacheim. Twenty Ausf. F2/G were delivered to Africa in July and August. Those were assigned to 15th and 21st Panzer Divisions which fought at El Alamein and Alam el Halfa in July, August and September 1942. It soon became clear that the new Panzer IV outperformed combat vehicles used by the Allies. As of August 30, 1942 5. Tank Battalion, 21st Panzer Division had 14 long-barreled Panzer IVs on strength, while 13 such vehicles served with the 8th Tank Battalion, 15th Panzer Division. By the end of the year 23 examples of the Ausf. F2/G were lost in combat, but in December 22 new examples

Pz.Kpfw. IV Ausf. H from 8th Company, II Battalion, 3rd Tank Regiment (2nd PzDiv.) during training in France in the early spring of 1944. A trident – division's insignia – is painted on the right forward section of the hull. [Bundesarchiv]

of the Ausf. G arrived in theater. The type was also among the combat vehicles which deployed in December 1942 to Tunisia, in service with 10th Panzer Division (16 tanks) and, later, "Hermann Göring" Division (8 machines). Although the joint German-Italian forces fought successfully at Kasserine Pass, the earlier defeat at El Alamein forced them to retreat back to Europe.

On June 22, 1941 the German Reich invaded the Soviet Union. At that time Panzer IVs in service with Panzerwaffe were exclusively short-barreled variants. Even in the early days of fighting on the Eastern Front it became clear that German tanks struggled to cope with Soviet KV heavy tanks and medium T-34 vehicles. Initially 88 mm FLAK guns remained the only effective weapon against the Soviet armor, but those weren't always available in most critical moments. It wasn't until the HEAT ammunition began to arrive at the front, followed by the Panzer IVs armed with KwK 40 guns that tables began to turn in favor of the Germans.

Table 2. Long-barreled Pz.Kpfw. IV tanks in service with panzer divisions in June and July 1942

Division	Total tanks	Pz.Kpfw. IV tanks	
		Total Pz.Kpfw. IV	Long-barreled vehicles
3rd PzDiv.	164	33	12
9th PzDiv.	144	21	12
11th PzDiv.	155	13	12
12th PzDiv.	58	10	4
14th PzDiv.	102	24	4
16th PzDiv.	100	27	12
22nd PzDiv.	176	22	11
23rd PzDiv.	138	27	10
24th PzDiv.	181	32	12
3rd Mot. Inf. Div.	54	8	8
16th Mot. Inf. Div	54	8	8
29th Mot. Inf. Div.	58	8	8
60th Mot. Inf. Div.	57	4	4
Mot. Inf. Div. "Grossdeuschland"	45	30	12
22nd PzBrig.	46	8	4

Source: T. Jentz, Panzertruppen. The Complete Guide to the Creation & Combat Employment of Germany's Tank Force 1933-1942, Atglen 1996.

Pz.Kpfw. IV Ausf. H from 5th Company, II Battalion, 12th SS Tank Regiment (12th PzDiv. SS "Hitlerjugend") during training near the Belgian town of Beverloo in January 1944. [Bundesarchiv]

Pz.Kpfw. IV Ausf. H from II Battalion, 12th SS Tank Regiment (12th PzDiv. SS "Hitlerjugend") during training at Beverloo, Belgium in January 1944. [Bundesarchiv]

Two Pz.Kpfw. IV Ausf. H tanks from I Platoon, 6th Company, II Battalion, 12th SS Tank Regiment (12th PzDiv. SS "Hitlerjugend") during training near the Belgian town of Beverloo in early 1944. [Bundesarchiv]

Table 3. Long-barreled Pz.Kpfw. IV tanks in service with panzer divisions on the eve of Operation Zitadelle			
Division	Total tanks	Pz.Kpfw. IV tanks	
		Total Pz.Kpfw. IV	Long-barreled vehicles
2nd PzDiv.	118	60	59
3rd PzDiv.	90	23	21
4th PzDiv.	101	80	79
5th PzDiv.	102	76	76
6th PzDiv.	117	32	32
7th PzDiv.	102	38	37
8th PzDiv.	104	22	14
9th PzDiv.	83	38	30
11th PzDiv.	113	26	25
12th. PzDiv.	83	37	36
13th PzDiv.	71	50	50
17th PzDiv.	67	32	31
18th PzDiv.	72	34	29
19th PzDiv.	81	38	36
20th PzDiv.	82	49	40
23rd PzDiv.	69	30	30
Pz.Gren.Div "Grossdeuschland"	132	68	63
Pz.Gren.Div SS "Leibstandarte SS Adolf Hitler"	116	67	67
Pz.Gren.Div SS "Das Reich"	145	33	33
Pz.Gren.Div SS "Totenkopf"	139	52	44
Pz.Gren.Div SS "Wiking"	45	17	16

Source: T. Jentz, Panzertruppen. The Complete Guide to the Creation & Combat Employment of Germany's Tank Force 1933-1942, Atglen 1996.

The first examples of the Ausf. F2 had their baptism of fire at Kharkov in May 1942 where they contributed to crushing a Soviet counteroffensive. More long-barreled "IVs" arrived in Russia in June and July 1942. Table 2 presents numbers of Panzer IV tanks in service with panzer divisions in that period.

February 1943 saw the capitulation of the German 6th Army at Stalingrad. Lost with it were 14th, 16th and 24th Panzer Divisions, as well as 3rd and 60th Motorized Infantry Divisions with a total of 34 Pz.Kpfw. IVs. On the eve of Operation Zitadelle in July 1943 the mainstay of German armored and motorized units were Pz.Kpfw. IV Ausf. G and H tanks. Details of the units equipped with those tanks that soon would go into battle at Kursk can be found in Table 3. Despite the arrival of new Pz.Kpfw. V tanks and combat support provided by heavy Pz.Kpfw. VI "Tigers", German forces suffered heavy losses in the battle.

The beginning of the end of German campaign on the Eastern Front came after defeats at Stalingrad and Kursk which resulted in huge losses in personnel and equipment from which the Third Reich never fully recovered for the rest of the war. The numbers of new armored vehicle, including Panzer IV tanks, making their way to the front were not enough to turn the tides in Germany's favor.

Another front where German forces were engaged in heavy fighting in 1943 was Italy. It began in July 1943 following Allied landings in Sicily. Stationed there were 15th and 29th Panzer Grenadier Divisions and Paratroop-Panzer Division "Herman Göring", which fielded a total of 78 long-barreled "IVs". Fifty two of those were lost in the fighting on the island.

Following the fall of Sicily, German forces retreated into mainland Italy. Operating there were the following units (numbers in parenthesis represent long-barreled Panzer IV tanks in service with each division): 16th PzDiv. (92), 24th PzDiv. (49), 26th PzDiv. (36), Paratroop-Panzer Division "Herman Göring" (31), 15th PzGren.Div. (15), 29th PzGren.Div. (none), 90th PzGren.Div. (37) and PzGren.Div. SS "Leibstandarte SS Adolf Hitler" (58). The latter, as well as the 24th PzDiv. were eventually deployed to the Eastern Front. In time more units were withdrawn and by the time the fighting in Italy had come to an end, only 26th PzDiv. and 29th and 90th PzGren. Div. remained in theater.

Pz.Kpfw. IV Ausf. H from 2nd SS Tank Regiment (2nd PzDiv. SS "Das Reich") on the move somewhere on the Eastern Front in December 1943. The vehicles wear single-tone, sand camouflage. Visible behind them are heavy Pz.Kpfw. VI "Tigers". [Bundesarchiv]

When the Allies landed in Normandy in June 1944 stationed in France were 2nd, 9th, 11th, 21st and 116th PzDiv., PzDiv. "Panzer Lehr", as well as 1st, 2nd and 12th PzDiv. SS. In total the Germans had 758 Panzer IV medium tanks in the area. Only between June 6 and July 8 as many as 197 vehicles of the type were lost in combat. Some of those losses were replaced by vehicles brought in by other units deployed to the front, including 9th and 10th PzDiv. SS, which operated a total of 85 Panzer IVs. In the meantime Allies went from strength to strength: German armored units were under a constant threat posed not only by enemy tanks, but also by air attacks.

German swan song was the operation "Wacht am Rhein" in the Ardennes, launched on December 16, 1944. As many as 391 Pz.Kpfw. IV tanks took part in the doomed counteroffensive.

CAMOUFLAGE AND MARKINGS

The first examples of Ausf. F2/G tanks delivered to frontline units were factory-sprayed with standard Panzer Grau paint. In winter conditions on the Eastern Front the dark-grey paint stood out against the snowy background making vehicles easy to detect. Based on the instruction issued on November 1941 such tanks were to receive overall white winter camouflage using removable white paint. Sometimes vehicles used in winter conditions on the Eastern Front were whitewashed using chalk.

On February 18, 1943, an order was issued to paint all newly assembled vehicles in a base coat of dark yellow (Wehrmacht Olive) paint. In some cases, especially in Sicily and in Italy, the factory-applied paint remained unmodified in front-line service. In general though, the coat was merely a base on which field camouflage was to be applied in patches of red-brown (Brun) and dark green (Dunkelgrün) or olive green (Olive Grün). The shape of patches, color scheme and color intensity all depended on the time of year in which the tank was used.

Vehicles in service with Deutsches Afrika Korps sported a different paint scheme. Initially the tanks wore standard European Panzer Grau, but it soon turned out that it wasn't suitable for African battlefield. A new order issued on March 17, 1941 required 2/3 of each tank to be covered with yellow brown paint (Gelb Braun), also known as the Afrika Korps Gelb. The remaining 1/3 of the surfaces were painted green grey (Grau). Sometimes, when paint supplies were slim, the only irregular patches of Gelb Braun were painted on top of the original Panzer Grau coat (exactly the opposite of what the instruction stipulated). In some cases Luftwaffe paint was used, or even paint captured from the British.

Another instruction specifying the paint scheme of tanks deployed to Africa was issued on March 25, 1942. Based on the new specification 2/3 of each vehicle was to be covered in dark brown paint (Sand-Brun), while the rest of the surfaces remained in Panzer Grau. Those proportions were hardly ever adhered to in practice.

German tanks wore Balkenkreuz measuring from 200 to 300 mm. When the first long-barreled Panzer IVs began to arrive, the standard Balkenkreuz had a shape of a thin white outline filled with black paint. The markings were painted on the front armor plate and on each side of the turret. On rare occasions Balkenkreuz markings were also added to the rear plate and the rear turret plate.

Tanks also wore unit insignia representing the division they were assigned to, but sometimes also regimental or battalion insignia. In some cases a single unit might have several types of insignia (e.g. 3rd, 11th or 18th PzDiv.). They could be either a geometric shape (15th PzDiv.), allegorical symbol (a ghost motif of 11th PzDiv.) or a coat of arms of the unit's home town (the Berlin bear of 3rd PzDiv.). The insignia were typically painted in yellow, although white and red versions could also be found. They were placed on the glacis, either side of the hull or turret and on the rear plate. Tanks serving with Afrika Korps had their own insignia – a palm tree with a swastika.

German armored units used a complex system of tactical markings. Those were usually painted white, red or yellow (sometimes using just white outlines) and placed on either side of the turret. In the three-digit format the first digit represented the company, second stood for platoon and third was the tank's individual number. The two-digit format was also used, but much less frequently – typically in independent or command units. The above markings were supplemented by letter "R" – used to identify regiment CO's vehicle, or Roman numerals "I", "II", "III" which were used by tanks of battalion commanders.

There were instances of individual names given to a tank by its crew, or commemorative inscriptions, perhaps celebrating a victory in one of the battles. A large flag of the Third Reich was draped over the engine deck as quick identification marking for friendly aircraft.

EXPORT

In order to maintain the desired quality of armored units of nations allied with the Third Reich (whose tanks, especially fighting on the Eastern front, were largely outclassed by enemy vehicles), the Germans launched military aid programs to supply their allies with combat equipment. In the case of the Panzer IV tanks, the following nations were on the list of the recipients:

- Bulgaria launched efforts to acquire Pz.Kpfw. IV as early as 1942. However, the first three examples of the tank weren't delivered until April 1943, followed by 11 more in May and 15 in June. Only two vehicles were delivered in August, while in September and November Bulgaria received 30 and 15 tanks,

Early production Pz.Kpf. IV Ausf. H "200". The vehicle, nicknamed "Grislybär", belonged to the CO of 2nd Company, I Battalion, 35th Tank Regiment (4th PzDiv.). Most likely Dmitrovsk area, September 1943. [Bundesarchiv]

A column of vehicles from I Battalion, 35th Tank Regiment (4th PzDiv.) on the move in Dmitrovsk area in September 1943. The vehicle in the foreground is early production example of Pz.Kpfw. IV Ausf. H. The type was first used on a larger scale during the Battle of Kursk. [Bundesarchiv]

respectively. In 1944 the country took delivery of 11 examples of the tank in January and 10 in February. In total Bulgaria received 97 Panzer IV tanks – some 29 Ausf. G, 65 Ausf. H models and three command vehicles. Ironically, the first time Bulgarian Panzer IVs saw combat was against German units marching into Bulgaria in September 1944. The fighting went on until November. The tanks then fought alongside Red Army units until April 1945.

- Hungary received 20 Ausf. F1 tanks in the spring of 1942, which went into service with Hungarian 1st Armored Division. Most of them were lost in combat o the Eastern Front. In August 1942 the country's armed forces took delivery of 4 Ausf. F2/G vehicles, followed by 12 Ausf. H tanks which were assigned to 2nd Armored Division. Further deliveries took place in November 1944 and in January 1945.

- Romania received their first 11 Ausf. G tanks as early as October 1942. Most of them were lost that winter in the fighting at the Don. Between 1943 and 1944 Romania received 106 Panzer IV tanks (F2/G, H and J models), including three command vehicles. They saw combat in Ukraine in 1943 assigned to Romanian 1st Armored Division. In August 1944 German forces began their retreat from Romania, taking with them Panzer IV tanks belonging to newly established 2nd Armored Division. Romanian Pz.Kpfw. IVs went on to fight their former allies – Germany and Hungary – alongside the Red Army. By the time the fighting drew to a close in April 1945 Romanian Panzer IV force had been reduced to a single tank.

- Italy received from 12 to 18 Pz.Kpfw. IV Ausf. H tanks in the summer of 1943. After Italy's surrender they were all repossessed by German units.

- Spain, although formally neutral, did fight on the side of the Germans against the Soviets (the Blue Division). In December 1943 Spanish 1st Armored Division received 20 Ausf. H tanks.

- Finland acquired 15 Pz.Kpfw. IV Ausf. J tanks in August 1944. In addition, the Third Reich supplied Finland with captured combat equipment.

- Croatia obtained 12 Pz.Kpfw. IV Ausf. G or Ausf. H vehicles in 1944. The tanks were used against Josip Tito's guerilla fighters.

CONCLUSION

Pz.Kpfw. IV was the mainstay of German medium tank force in the second half of the war. Along the Pz.Kpfw. V "Panther" it was also the most widely manufactured medium tank used by the Panzerwaffe. Based on the original specifications, the vehicle was to be employed in combat support role and in the early stages of the war it served that purpose quite well. However, in the face of the rapid improvement of armored weapons technology, which gave rise to better armed and heavily armored enemy tanks, Panzer IV needed a facelift. In the end the most effective marks of the tank proved to be the late models armed with long 75 mm guns, which gave Panzer IV a fighting chance against enemy armor.

Once the long-barreled Ausf. F2/G models began to arrive at battlefields in the East and in Africa, they gave Panzerwaffe a much needed second wind. Panzer IV remained the basic medium tank used by German armored units even after the "Panther" had entered service. It needs to be mentioned,

A well-camouflaged Pz.Kpfw. IV Ausf. H from an unidentified unit photographed in northern France in the summer of 1944. [Bundesarchiv]

however that the design came very close to being withdrawn front frontline use even before the end of the war. In early 1943 German high command and Hitler himself insisted that production of Panzer IV tanks should be discontinued in favor of the new "Panther" medium tank and heavy Pz.Kpfw. VI "Tiger". It was only thanks to Heinz Guderian's intervention as the Inspector of General of Panzerwaffe that the production of the "IV" could continue. Later there were plans to mate the Panzer IV Ausf. H and J chassis with a standard "Panther" turret or with the Schmalturm turret.

Perhaps the best way to truly assess the Panzer IV's worth as a combat vehicle would be by comparison to tanks of a similar class in service with the Third Reich's adversaries. In the case of the USSR the obvious candidate for such a comparison is the T-34/76, the 1943 model being perhaps most suitable. The Western Allies are represented by the M4A1 Sherman, manufactured between February 1942 and the end of 1943. Key data is summarized in Table 4.

In terms of weight Panzer IV was lighter than the competition – by three tons compared to the T-34 and by five tons compared to the M4A1. The German tank was also longer than the other two – 7.02 m compared to 5.92 m (T-34) and 6.2 m (Sherman). It wasn't as wide as the Russian tank 2.88 m compared to 3 m), but a bit wider than the Sherman (2.67). The highest of the three was the Sherman (2.94 m) with Panzer IV just behind (2.68 m) and the T-34 coming third at 2.4 m.

Table 4. Comparison of key technical and tactical characteristics

	Pz.Kpfw. IV Ausf. H-J	T-34 model 1943	M4A1 Sherman
Crew	5	4	5
Weight	25 t	28 t	30 t
Length	7.02 m	5.92 m	6.20 m
Width	2.88 m	3.00 m	2.67 m
Height	2.68 m	2.40 m	2.94 m
Ground clearance	0.40 m	0.40 m	0.43 m
Engine/cooling system	gasoline, liquid-cooled	Diesel, liquid-cooled	gasoline, air-cooled
Engine power	265 hp	500 hp	350 hp
Road speed	38-40 km/h	55 km/h	39 km/h
Range (road/off-road)	210-320/130-210 km	300/250 km	193/N/A
Fuel capacity	470-680 dm³	594 dm³	662 dm³
Armament	1 x 75 mm, 2 machine guns	1 x 76.2 mm, 2 machine guns	1 x 75 mm, 1 x 12.7 mm, 2 machine guns
Ammunition supply	87 gun rounds, 3,150 machine gun rounds	100 gun rounds, 2,646 machine gun rounds	90 gun rounds, 300 12.7 mm rounds, 4,750 machine gun rounds
Hull armor	front from 20 to 80 mm, sides and rear from 14 to 30 mm	front, sides and rear up to 45 mm	front 51 mm, sides and rear 38 mm
Turret armor	front 50 mm, sides and rear 30 mm	front 40-52 mm, sides and rear 52 mm	front 51-76 mm, sides and rear 51 mm
Gradient	30°	35°	30°
Fording	80 cm	140 cm	100 cm
Trench	230 cm	250 cm	230 cm
Vertical obstacle	60 cm	73 cm	60 cm

Source: M. Bariatinskij, T-34, Warszawa 2007; M. Fiszer, J. Gruszczyński, *Czołg średni M4 Sherman*, "Nowa Technika Wojskowa. Numer Specjalny" 2008, nr 1; T. Jentz, H. Doyle, *Panzerkampfwagen IV. Grosstraktor to Panzerbefehlswagen*, Darlington 1997.

Early production Pz.Kpfw. IV Ausf. H from an unknown Panzerwaffe unit negotiating anti-tank trench somewhere on the Eastern Front. August or September 1943. The vehicle wears a single-tone grey-sand paint scheme. [Bundesarchiv]

German Ausf. H and J models were protected by 20 to 80 mm front plates, 20 -30 mm side armor (plus additional spaced armor) and 14 to 20 mm in the rear. The turret's front and gun mantlet were protected by 50 mm armor, while sides and rear were made of 30 mm plates. The xxx featured 51 mm front hull plates and 38 mm side and rear plates. Its turret's front was protected by 51 to 76 mm armor, while side and rear plates were 51 mm thick. The Russian tank's armor was the weakest of the three: hull front, sides and rear – 45 mm, front of the turret – from 40 to 52 mm, sides and rear of the turret – 52 mm.

Based on the above data, one might be tempted to think that the German tank was greatly superior to its adversaries, especially due to its glacis protection – the area that's most vulnerable to enemy fire. However, when the shape of the armor is considered, this advantage becomes less straightforward. The T-34 featured sloped armor, which meant the plates didn't need to be very thick to be effective, which resulted in weight saving. Sherman's front armor wasn't as radically sloped as the T-34, but it was still shaped at a decent angle. The German tank, on the other hand, featured either vertical armor plates (especially on hull sides) or only slightly inclined. This resulted in the vehicle's characteristic boxy look and required a thicker armor for adequate protection.

Pz.Kpfw. IV Ausf. H and J were armed with long-barreled 75 mm main guns with a supply of 87 rounds of ammunition. Armor piercing rounds could penetrate 91 mm of armor at 500 m and 82 mm at 1,000 m. At those distances it was therefore effective against the front hull and turret armor of its adversaries, let alone their side armor plates. KEP rounds performed even better and were capable of penetrating 108 mm of armor at 500 m or 85 mm at 1,000 m. HEAT rounds used by German tanks had enough punch to penetrate from 70 to 100 mm of armor (depending on the type of round) at any distance.

A column of Pz.Kfw. IV Ausf. H tanks from 6th Company, II Battalion, 29th Tank Regiment (12th PzDiv.) on the move, most likely in Bialystok area, Poland in July 1944. Notice an additional armor plate mounted on the roof of the lead vehicle's turret. [Bundesarchiv]

This early production Pz.Kpfw. IV Ausf. H from an unidentified unit was photographed on the Eastern Front in the winter of 1943. Clearly visible is the Zusatzpanzerung attached to the hull's front plate. [Bundesarchiv]

The Sherman's M3 gun was also a 75 mm weapon with a supply of 90 rounds of ammunition. The shells could penetrate 72 mm of armor at 457 m. The T-34's 76.2 mm gun (with a supply of 100 shells) fired projectiles that could deal with 70 – 90 mm armor plate at 500 m and 60 mm at 1,000 m.

The T-34 was the only one of the three vehicles compared here that used a fuel-efficient, liquid-cooled Diesel engine developing 500 hp. The other two were powered by gasoline engines, either liquid-cooled (Panzer IV, 265 hp) or air-cooled (Sherman, 350 hp). The T-34 was also the fastest of the lot, with a top speed of up to 55 km/h. The other two vehicles had comparable top speeds ranging from 39 to 40 km/h.

Initially the American tank had the highest fuel capacity of 662 dm^3, compared to 594 and 470 in Russian and German tanks, respectively. However, the last production version of Panzer IV had a fuel tank capacity increased to 680 dm^3. At the same time Sherman had the worst fuel economy figures of all three tanks, which translated into a range of only 193 km on road surfaces. The T-34 could travel 300 km on roads or 250 km cross-country. Panzer IV, depending on the version, had a range from 210 to 320 km (road) or 130 – 210 km (cross-country). The T-34 was the best performer in terms of total fuel capacity vs. fuel economy.

American and German tanks were comparable terrain performers. Both could negotiate 2.3 m trenches, 0.6 m vertical obstacles and could climb gradients of up to 30°. In the case of the T-34 the numbers were as follows: 2.5 m, 0.73 m and 35°. However, the Panzer IV was comprehensively beaten by its adversaries in fording capability: it could only negotiate a 0.8 m water obstacle. The Sherman and T-34 were much better in this respect – 1.4 m (T-34) and 1.00 m (M4A1).

As can be seen, Panzer IV had decent characteristics, on par with its main rivals or even better, in some areas. However, its main weakness had nothing to do with technical specs, but rather with the limited capacity of the Reich's industry to build the tank in large enough numbers. A total of 1,930 examples of the Ausf. F2/G vehicles were delivered, 2,322 Ausf. H tanks and 3,160 Ausf. J models – 7,412 vehicles in total. Partially to blame were disruption in tank production caused by Hitler's decision to use some of the Pz.Kpfw. IV chassis for assault guns – a move fiercely criticized by Guderian.

In the meantime U.S. factories churned out no fewer than 6,281 M4A1 tanks (out of 33,671 examples armed with the 75 mm gun and a grand total 49,000 of all Sherman vehicles), while Russia produced 15,833 T-34s, model 1943. A total number of all T-34 versions armed with the 76.2 mm gun delivered to armored units reached over 35,000 vehicles.

Nonetheless, Pz.Kpfw. IV represented on all fronts of the war as a true core of German armored units, fully deserves its reputation as the workhorse of Panzerwaffe. The fact that the tanks chassis was successfully used for conversion into a series of special purpose vehicles (such as "Hummel" assault guns or Jagdpazer IV and "Hornisse" tank destroyers) is perhaps the best testament to the design's versatility. It was also

Pz.Kpfw. IV Ausf. H from II Battalion, "Grossdeutschland" Tank Regiment, (Pz.Gren.Div. "Grossdeutschland") operating in the Kirovgrad area in December 1943. The vehicles had been whitewashed using white removable paint. Spare track links served as extra armor protection. [Bundesarchiv]

a potent combat vehicle that went on to serve with armed forces of a number of nations years after the war had ended. For example, Panzer IV tanks acquired after the war by Syria were successfully used during the so called "War over Water" with Israel in 1965 and in the Six-Day War two years later.

SELECTED BIBLIOGRAPHY

Bariatinskij Michaił, *T-34*, Warszawa 2007.
Battistelli Paolo, *Niemieckie dywizje pancerne – front wschodni 1941-1943*, Warszawa 2010.
Chamberlain Peter, Doyle Hilary, *Encyclopaedia Of German Tanks Of World War Two: The Complete Illustrated Directory of German Battle Tanks, Armoured Cars, Self-propelled Guns and Semi-tracked Vehicles, 1933-45*, bmw 1999.
Culver Bruce, Murphy Bill, *Panzer Colors. Camouflage of the German Panzer Forces 1939-1945*, Carrolton 1976.
Culver Bruce, *Panzer Colors. Markings of the German Panzer Forces 1939-1945*, Carrolton 1978.
Doyle Hilary, Friedli Lucas, Jentz Thomas, *Panzerkampfwagen IV Ausf. H/Ausf. J, 1943 to 1945*, Boyds 2016.
Fiszer Michał, Gruszczyński Jerzy, *Czołg średni M4 Sherman*, „Nowa Technika Wojskowa. Numer Specjalny" 2008, nr 1.
Fleischer Wolfgang, *Die Deutschen Kampfwagen Kanonen 1935-1945*, Wölfersheim-Berstadt 1996.
Fleischer Wolfgang, *Panzerkampfwagen IV. Rückgrat der deutschen Panzerverbände*, Wölfersheim-Berstadt 2002.
Gładysiak Łukasz, Karmieh Samir, *Panzer IV Ausf. H and Ausf. J, vol. I*, Lublin 2015.
Guderian Heinz, *Wspomnienia żołnierza*, Warszawa 2013
Jędrzejewski Dariusz, Lalak Zbigniew, *Sojusznicy Panzerwaffe, część I*, Warszawa 1998.
Jentz Thomas, Doyle Hilary, *Panzerkampfwagen IV. Grosstraktor to Panzerbefehlswagen*, Darlington 1997.
Jentz Thomas, *Panzertruppen. The Complete Guide to the Creation & Combat Employment of Germany's Tank Force 1933-1942*, Atglen 1996.
Jentz Thomas, *Panzertruppen. The Complete Guide to the Creation & Combat Employment of Germany's Tank Force 1943-1945*, Atglen 1996.
Ledwoch Janusz, *PzKpfw IV vol II*, Warszawa 2001.
Ledwoch Janusz, *PzKpfw IV vol I-II*, Warszawa 2007.
Mucha Krzysztof, Parada George, Styrna Wojciech, *Panzer IV Sd.Kfz. 161, vol. I*, Lublin 2002.
Niehorster Leo, *Mechanized Army Divisions (22 June 1941)*, Crownhill 2007.
Niehorster Leo, *Mechanized Army Divisions (28 June 1942)*, Crownhill 2007.
Niehorster Leo, *Mechanized Army Divisions (4 July 1943)*, Crownhill 2007.
Perrett Brian, *Panzerkampfwagen IV Medium Tank 1936-1945*, Oxford 1999.
Scheibert Horst, *Panzerkampfwagen IV*, Friedberg 1975.
Skotnicki Mariusz, *Czołgi średnie Pz.Kpfw. IV Ausf. F1 i F2 – najlepsze krótkolufowe i pierwsze długolufowe „czwórki"*, „Nowa Technika Wojskowa. Numer Specjalny" 2010, nr 1.
Spielberger Walter, *Panzer IV & Its Variants*, Atglen 1993
Spielberger Walter, *Panzerkampfwagen IV (F2)*, Surrey 1967.
Spielberger Walter, *Panzerkampfwagen IV*, Windsor 1972.
Trojca Waldemar, *Sd.Kfz. 161 Pz.Kpfw. IV Ausf. F/F2/G, vol. 1*, Katowice-Speyer 2002.
Trojca Waldemar, *Sd.Kfz. 161 Pz.Kpfw. IV Ausf. F/F2/G, vol. 2*, Katowice-Speyer 2005.
Zaloga Steven, *Panzer IV vs Sherman. France 1944*, Oxford 2015.

ENDNOTES

[1] This part of the designation will be omitted in the text to follow (author's note).

Two close-ups of Pz.Kpfw. IV Ausf. H "1251" from II Battalion, "Grossdeutschland" Tank Regiment (Pz.Gren Div. "Grossdeutschland"). Kirovgrad area, December 1943. Armor plates, mud guards and spaced armor around the turret had all been treated with Zimmerit. [Bundesarchiv]

Table 5. Tactical and technical characteristics of the Pz.Kpfw. IV Ausf. F2/G, H and J			
	Pz.Kpfw. IV Ausf. F2/G	Pz.Kpfw. IV Ausf. H	Pz.Kpfw. IV Ausf. J
Crew:	5	5	5
Weight:	23,600 kg	25,000 kg	25,000 kg
Dimensions:			
Length	6,630 mm	7,020 mm	7,020 mm
Width	2,880 mm	2,880 mm	2,880 mm
Height	2,680 mm	2,680 mm	2,680 mm
Ground clearance	400 mm	400 mm	400 mm
Engine:	Maybach HL 120 TRM	Maybach HL 120 TRM	Maybach HL 120 TRM
Engine power:	265 hp at 2,600 rpm	265 hp at 2,600 rpm	265 hp at 2,600 rpm
Speed:			
- max	40 km/h	38 km/h	38 km/h
- average - road	up to 25 km/h	up to 25 km/h	up to 25 km/h
- average – cross-country	up to 20 km/h	up to 20 km/h	up to 20 km/h
Range:			
- road	up to 210 km	up to 210 km	up to 320 km
- cross-country	up to 130 km	up to 130 km	up to 210 km
Fuel capacity (dm^3):	470 dm^3	470 dm^3	680 dm^3
Armament:			
- main gun	7,5 cm KwK 40 L/43 (later 7,5 cm KwK 40 L/48)	7,5 cm KwK 40 L/48	7,5 cm KwK 40 L/48
- machine guns	2 x MG-34	2 x MG-34	2 x MG-34
Ammunition supply:			
- main gun	87 shells	87 shells	87 shells
- machine guns	3,150 rounds	3,150 rounds	3,150 rounds
Armor:			
- hull	10-50 mm (up to 80 mm with additional plate)	10-80 mm	10-80 mm
- turret	10-50 mm	10-50 mm	10-50 mm
Track width (mm):	400 mm	400 mm	400 mm
Number of track links:	99	99	99
Terrain obstacles:			
- gradient:	30°	30°	30°
- fording:	80 cm	80 cm	80 cm
- trench:	230 cm	230 cm	230 cm
- vertical obstacles:	60 cm	60 cm	60 cm

Source: : T. Jentz, H. Doyle, *Panzerkampfwagen IV. Grosstraktor to Panzerbefehlswagen*, Darlington 1997; H. Doyle, L. Friedli, T. Jentz, *Panzerkampfwagen IV Ausf. H/Ausf. J, 1943 to 1945*, Boyds 2016.

A pair of Pz.Kpfw. IV Ausf. H tanks from 3rd and 4th Company, I Battalion, 21st Tank Regiment (20th PzDiv.). The vehicles were destroyed by advancing Soviet troops in Bobruisk area in late June 1944. [Robert Wróblewski's collection]

A column of Pz.Kpfw. IV Ausf. H tanks from an unidentified unit on the move. Eastern Front, 1943/44. All crew members wear insulated winter uniforms (Wendbarer Winteranzug) issued to all Wehrmacht troops. [Bundesarchiv]